Modern Mothering

Other Books by the Author

Daily Affirmations for Parents: How to Nurture Your Children and Renew Yourself during the Ups and Downs of Parenthood

Daily Affirmations for Forgiving and Moving On: Powerful Inspiration for Personal Change

Journey Through Womanhood: Meditations from Our Collective Soul

The Magic of Forgiveness: Emotional Freedom and Transformation at Mid-Life

The Quiet Voice of Soul: How to Find Meaning in Ordinary Life

The Soul's Companion: Connecting with the Soul through Daily Meditations

It's My Life: A Power Journal for Teens

Heartwounds: The Impact of Unresolved Trauma and Grief on Relationships

Trauma and Addiction: Ending the Cycle of Pain through Emotional Literacy

Drama Games: Techniques for Self-Development

The Drama Within: Psychodrama and Experiential Therapy

The Living Stage: A Step by Step Guide to Psychodrama, Sociometry, and Experiential Group Therapy

Modern Mothering

How to Teach Kids to Say What They Feel
and Feel What They Say

Tian Dayton, Ph.D.

A Crossroad Book
The Crossroad Publishing Company
New York

The Crossroad Publishing Company
www.CrossroadPublishing.com

Printed in the United States of America

The text of this book is set in 10/13.5 Benguiat.
The display faces are Liberty and Benguiat Gothic.

Library of Congress Cataloging-in-Publication Data

Dayton, Tian.
    Modern mothering : how to teach children to say what they feel
and feel what they say / Tian Dayton.
        p. cm.
    Includes bibliographical references.
    ISBN 0-8245-2340-7 (alk. paper)
    1. Child psychology. 2. Child rearing. 3. Child rearing – Religious
aspects. 4. Mother and child. 5. Mother and child – Religious
aspects. I. Title.
HQ772.D35 2005
649'.1 – dc22

                                                        2005025670

1 2 3 4 5 6 7 8 9 10   10 09 08 07 06 05

To my most darling Marina and Alex,
who woke my heart and mind to the real dance of life,
and to my ever and always beloved Brandt,
without whom, after all,
none of this would have been possible

Contents

Contents 7

Motherhood
A soul journey

We can do no great things,
only small things with great love.
— Mother Teresa

Motherhood was my trip to the moon, my journey through inner space. It took me to some places I never knew existed and let me revisit others, seeing them through new and much improved eyes. It stretched, challenged, and moved my inner world forward in a way that nothing ever had before. It has been my great adventure, the one that left me standing breathless at its sheer size and proportion, that tucked me in at night warm and cozy and woke me up in the morning with a heart full of a particular kind of joy that I never knew was possible. These feelings of love, protection, and emotional connection stretched my heart into a new shape, patted and pulled at it with tiny, chubby hands and tucked it back into my chest all freshened up. Never has an experience so shuffled my insides around, redone my priorities or moved me consistently beyond my own limitations.

Motherhood just popped up on me and took over my life. Nothing was mine anymore, not my time, my body, my mind, or my heart. Motherhood blended me and spilled me out all in a new order. And each moment that I thought I couldn't hang on any longer or deepen my capacity for love and joy another millimeter, motherhood showed me I could. My babies, my soul, my heart, and my good fortune. My gifts from God, my platter of riches. The love. Who could have ever told me about this kind of love? Who could have explained to me that once this thing happened everything else would move to a different place, sail down the scale of importance because nothing compared to the importance of them? That this experience could liberate me from my own smallness and teach me how to be?

The Core of This Book

The mother's lap is the child's first classroom.

— Hindu proverb

This book circles around a few basic themes. They have been the guiding principles of my own journey of motherhood and those of many of my clients and friends over the years. The sorority of motherhood bonds women at a profound level, whatever race, color, or creed; we understand each other and share an experience that is larger than all of us. It even bonds us with the animal kingdom. I see shades of my own experience in deer, horses, dogs, and cats. Even birds guard their young with a ferocity and devotion that I can intuitively relate to. But to be a human mother allows us to go beyond our biological mandate and to draw on our intellects in order to use the experience of nurturing children as a vehicle for our own soul growth. So the first theme of this book is that *motherhood is a spiritual path*. Second is that it is an *opportunity to heal our own pasts*. Third is that it is a lifelong commitment that *transforms us on the inside forever*. And the fourth is that *we wire our children's emotional (i.e., limbic) systems a day at a time* through the nature and quality of our connection with them.

Motherhood is a *spiritual path* because as mothers, we virtually touch souls with these little beings. We learn to give *and* receive, to open our hearts to love, abundance, vulnerability, and pain; to care and be cared about. We develop ever increasing amounts of patience, perseverance, trust, and tolerance. To give for the sake of giving, to love for the pleasure of loving, and to put someone else's welfare before our own. Motherhood reorganizes our insides, our outsides, and if we let it, our relationship to the divine order of things. We enter into the mystery as the spirit becomes flesh in the form of our children; we experience God's presence. The love we feel for our children, along with the profound need we have to protect and nurture this life, is so overpowering that we have to look to spiritual solutions alongside human ones to keep from going mad with worry or to contain and share our joy. We learn the meaning of surrender. Protect this life, God, which means more to me than my own, care for this child of *ours,* love her, nurture him, tamp down a path through the world that she or he can walk in safety and security. Give us your blessing and hold us in your light each and every day.

We are *transformed on the inside* because as mothers, we learn to experience deeper levels of connection with ourselves and others. It can give us the courage to perceive, confront, and experience those deeper layers that we all have, instead of running from them; we bring literacy, insight, and understanding where once there may have been silence. This is one of the ways we stretch and grow emotionally. We cannot name an emotional experience before we have had it. The sheer depth and breadth of our inner world and our ability to connect to the inner world of another person literally expands through motherhood. The intensity of our intimacy with our children gives us new types of emotional experiences within both the self and our relationships. We truly stretch our capacity to feel and renew and rework our ability to form meaningful bonds. When we open ourselves to the experience of deep love, that all-consuming feeling can seep into the drafty cracks of our hearts and vibrate in the missing spaces. It can transform emptiness into a spiritual void rich with meaning and potential.

It is a spiritual paradox that we "lose the self to find it." In motherhood we do lose the self. And we need to find it also, to find that balance between allowing both ourselves and those we love the feeling of having a self. We recognize that if we don't nourish and continue to expand and explore our own self, we risk letting a part of us go hungry. But when we give from an empty container, eventually we resent it and want a self in return from someone else. For healthy relationships, we need to allow both ourselves and our children to experience a sense of self *while* in each other's presence.

Motherhood is an opportunity to *heal our pasts* because our children awaken the sleeping child in us. And in so doing, we

experience not only a rebirth of wonder but, through deep connection, we also touch upon those unhealed wounds that lie
dormant within us. We feel or refeel what has been living inside of us without our even knowing it. As we experience these
forgotten parts of self, we have the opportunity to come alive
again, to become more whole. Our motherhood acts as a window into our own experience of being a child. The feelings of
dependency and vulnerability that we share with our spouses
and children naturally recall to the surface those lessons on
intimacy, good, bad, and indifferent, that we learned in our
relationships with our own parents and siblings.

Most of us do have some unresolved issues floating around.
But we need to make a conscious connection as to why we're
feeling what we're feeling when those issues do get triggered,
otherwise, chances are we will "act out" without awareness. We
will pass on the unconscious pain inside us that is being re-
stimulated by projecting it into our present-day relationships
and not recognize that the intensity of it belongs elsewhere,
to another time and place. But if we let our mothering illumi-
nate our own issues around connection and allow ourselves
to use what we're feeling to enhance our own understanding
of ourselves and our relationship issues, then we heal a little
more each day and we give that gift to our children. It is what
remains hidden and unconscious that tends to exacerbate our
knee-jerk reactions in parenting. Once we thaw out our inner
world and take a look at it, we can usually figure out why we're
acting how we're acting. And in liberating ourselves from the
unhealed parts of our pasts we liberate our children from them
also, because our past still lives in the present through us.

And here's how we *wire and shape our children's limbic systems.* Each tiny interaction between the mother and child lays
down wiring that shapes our children's neurological network.
Then the child grows ever so slightly and relates to us using
and experimenting with this bit of new growth. We, in turn, relate back to them and new wiring continues to build and be
laid down. This constant interaction evolves and expands the
growing child's neural network. All of this process of interactive

building creates a fluid rather than a static picture of childhood development. Not nature *vs.* nurture but nature *and* nurture in constant interaction. This constantly evolving neural wiring becomes part of what is called our limbic or our emotional system. Our "early emotional experiences knit long-lasting patterns into the very fabric of the brain's neural networks" (Lewis et al. 2001). Our emotional life is physical; it imprints itself on our bodies. The limbic system is the body/mind system through which we experience and regulate our emotions. This is why it is so important. The time and energy that we invest in our children while they are young is an investment that pays itself back throughout their lives and ours. It is during children's young years that we build the foundation for emotional intelligence, which is at the core of both emotional literacy and cognitive intelligence. Without this solid infrastructure, children are operating at a deficit and with it they have a solid architecture upon which to build the person they are always in the process of becoming. This newest research echoes the most ancient knowledge. As mothers we shape the emotional, psychological, and physiological world of our children in profound and lasting ways. The "mother's lap" really is "the child's first classroom."

What Does Our Limbic System Do?

The limbic system "sets the mind's emotional tone, filters external events through internal states (creates emotional coloring), tags events as internally important, stores highly charged emotional memories, modulates motivation, controls appetite and sleep cycles, promotes bonding and directly processes the sense of smell and modulates libido" (Amen 1998). We learn self-regulation from being around an adept external regulator. As mothers we are ideally suited to teach self-regulation to our children.

Putting Words to Feelings and Feelings to Words

What we mean by emotional literacy

In the last decade or so, science has discovered a tremendous amount about the role emotions play in our lives. Researchers have found that even more than IQ, your emotional awareness and abilities to handle feelings will determine your success and happiness in all walks of life, including family relationships.

— John Gottman, *Raising an Emotionally Intelligent Child*

Emotional literacy is really the ability to think about what we're feeling. It is the outgrowth of sound emotional development. And sound emotional development does not come out of nowhere. It is built a day at a time through a close and caring relationship with generally a parent or grandparent. It all starts with creating a safe enough space so that we can actually feel what we're feeling, such as the safe relational space between a mother and child can provide — what psychologists refer to as "a holding environment." We learn the meaning of closeness and distance by making our mothers the center of our world and measuring distance against her. We learn to assign words to particular emotions as she defines them for us when they arise. We learn to regulate our emotional states by modeling hers and by being wooed from the emotional edges toward a center that mother and child create together. Then we need to incorporate this "holding" environment that we set up with our primary caretakers into ourselves and walk around with it. Once we can essentially experience or momentarily "hold" our emotions we can get to the next steps, which are to name them, think about them, and "talk them out." But this happens gradually, over time. The body/mind is an integrated system that develops in exquisite synchronization. There is much emotional, psychological, and physiological terrain to cover before abstract concepts can be boiled down into words and those words can be used as building blocks for personal understanding, communication, and emotional literacy. And that's what this book is about: the ground that we cover with our children that allows them to be emotionally sound, intelligent, and literate little beings.

———— ((◦)) ————

Emotions are the glue that holds the
cells of the organism together.
— Candace Pert, *EQ Today,* Spring 1999

———— ((◦)) ————

The ability to *feel, name, think, and talk about emotions* is really the core of emotional literacy. That's why this holding environment is absolutely essential. If we can't tolerate the experience of feeling our feelings, there is no such thing as emotional literacy, emotional intelligence, or emotional understanding. Most of emotional literacy goes awry at just this level. If we don't feel safe or strong enough inside of ourselves to experience our internal states, we may want to run away from them, shut them down, or act them out in destructive ways. Running can mean anything from repressing, rewriting, denying, or dissociating. Shutting down is exactly that, turning off or going numb. Acting out is when we *act out* rather than *talk out* our feelings. Maybe we're angry, sad, and scared and we can't hold those feelings, own and experience them as our own, and we want to get rid of them instead. Our attempts to get rid of what we're feeling are an anathema to emotional literacy; they stop it in its tracks. When we block or act out rather than talk out our emotions we have nothing to work with. We can't get to "reasoning and thinking" because we have nothing to reason or think about. We need the experience of that safe emotional space with our families to help us learn that we won't die of strong feelings and that our relationships won't disappear if we allow our genuine selves to emerge in a manageable fashion. It is when our emotions come out without awareness or understanding, i.e., when they get *acted out* rather than *talked out* that they cause the most trouble.

Research into emotions is a fairly recent phenomenon. Previously our research dollars went to the cognitive growth of children. How do they learn to read earlier, become mathematical or musical at a young age? But the neurological research that has been booming onto the scene for the past decade or more points to the critical role of emotions in such areas as self-regulation, decision making, capacity for relationships, ability to find passion and meaning in life, and, yes, learning of all kinds. A calm, emotionally well-regulated child is able to learn more easily. Emotions are at the core of some of our most basic functions.

Emotions Are Key to Our Survival

Emotions are key to our survival. They are what fuels a mother's undying attachment so that she will not abandon her young, what alerts us to danger so we can get out of harm's way, and what we experience as pain upon separation. Nature operates on a punishment/reward system. This means we are rewarded with cascades of "feel-good chemicals" by experiences that aid survival and punished with "stress chemicals" during experiences that run counter to it. So key are *family* and *community* to survival that nature has rewarded close connection and made separation hurt. Not accidentally, the opiates that are our biological reward system are turned on by *touch*. The "opiates of attachment" or "brain fertilizers" that are turned on by the kind of touching and closeness between the mother and child strengthen connections between neurons in the brain that literally make someone more intelligent, fit, and eventually a more successful adult. They are food for the brain and body. Without these molecules coursing through us, the brain cannot connect up properly. This is why nature rewards mother/child intimacy so strongly by making it a pleasurable experience, because without it, our children can't survive and thrive.

See Me, Feel Me, Touch Me, Heal Me: The Power of Sensory Learning

Our babies find their mother's face the most interesting and absorbing sight in the world. When we turn our caring and cooing attention toward them we are double coding information. Through her senses she is absorbing the experience of relatedness, and we are attaching emotional meaning to that interactive space. After birth there is a rapid expansion of neuronal connections in our baby's brain as she begins to take in information through her senses. These form the basis for learning. Our babies like to use many of their senses at the same time and we are a perfect multimedia experience for them. They learn about being in the world by watching our faces. How are we reacting and what are does our reaction mean?

The capacity to feel, to be empathic, attuned, and engaged with our children during all points of their development, is at the crux of being a good mother. Helping our children to develop the ability to tolerate their strong feelings and translate those feelings into words so that they can be held out in the intellectual space between parent and child, thought about, and reasoned through is central to developing the ability to integrate our personalities and regulate our body/mind emotional systems.

Most of pathology, if you think about it, comes from running from what we really feel, from hiding what is really going on inside of us from others and eventually from ourselves and developing elaborate defenses, acting out behaviors, secret lives, or addictions to act out what we can't tolerate feeling and talking out. But if we develop the skills of emotional literacy, we can grow in understanding ourselves and another person rather than the opposite, which is being separated by our strong emotions.

How the Way We Handle Our Children Can Nourish Them Emotionally

The sight of our faces and the calming sound of our voice combined with gentle caresses help the baby in our arms to feel safe and secure. These sensations have to power both to stimulate and sooth them and they learn this so naturally in our arms as we introduce ourselves and the world to them bit by digestible bit, as we act as their external modulator, our hand gently on the rheostat of life adjusting the volume and intensity to what is right for our child at any given moment. "A curious, calm and regulated baby is by definition a secure baby" (Greenspan 1999) — one who is learning what the world is made of and how and what to feel about it. This coding of information actually lays down new neural pathways on which further learning becomes strengthened.

We can help our child develop emotional variety and stability through the way we handle them, and the more senses involved in this experience, the more he or she will remember it. This enriched emotional environment doesn't mean we buy more toys or take more classes or hang more mobiles. It means we spend more time because we're more important to our baby than any other experience. We're the enriched environment.

I am writing to you because I believe in mothering with all my heart. What we give to our children reverberates through the generations. Our children come into this world literally through us, wanting our love and nurturing more than anything else. How we see them seeps into their emotional pores. How we hold them imprints itself on their bodies and how we think about them lays down the foundation of core beliefs that they build upon throughout their lives and pass along to their children. Nothing could be more important.

Emotional Development Is the Foundation for Intelligence and Cognitive Skills

Studies [are] suggesting that pushing baby to learn words, numbers, colors and shapes too early forces the child to use lower-level thinking processes, rather than develop his or her learning ability. It's like a pony trick at the circus: When the pony paws the ground to "count" to three, it's really not counting; it's simply performing a stunt. Such "tricks" are not only not helpful to a baby's learning process, they are potentially harmful. Tufts University child psychologist David Elkind, Ph.D., makes it clear that putting pressure on a child to learn information sends the message that he or she needs to "perform" to gain the parents' acceptance, and it can dampen natural curiosity.

Instead, focus on building baby's emotional skills. "Emotional development is not just the foundation for important capacities such as intimacy and trust," says Stanley Greenspan, M.D., clinical professor of psychiatry and pediatrics at George Washington University Medical School and author of the new comprehensive book *Building Healthy Minds*. "It is also the foundation of intelligence and a wide variety of cognitive skills. At each stage of development, emotions lead the way, and learning facts and skills follow. Even math skills, which appear [to be] strictly an impersonal cognition, are initially learned through the emotions: 'A lot' to a 2-year-old, for example, is more than he would expect, whereas 'a little' is less than he wants."

—Joanna Lipari, Psy.D., "Four Things You Need to Know about Your Baby,"
Psychology Today, July 2000

Our children also teach us about what it means to be "real," in the "Velveteen Vernacular," to rub off our rough edges and learn to be human. They are constantly reminding us that there is no such thing as controlling another person, as getting them to behave or do exactly what we want them to do or getting a situation to go just as we want it to go. When we want them to stand they sit, when we want them to hurry, they slow down, and when we want them to be polite and impress our friends they hide behind our skirt or throw a tantrum. They make us learn to let go. They do not experience time as we do and consequently time in their presence tends to take on other qualities, to morph into and out of wormholes in space that can make a minute feel like an hour or an hour feel like a minute. If we truly want to enter our children's world and share time and space with them, we will have to slow down and become a part of the eternity from which they have come and to which they call us. Being present to the moment, living a day at a time, any saint or sage would say is a path into the mystery of creation and the experience of God. This is holy ground we stand on with our children, nothing less. Try as we might we cannot rush life. Our children will grow in their time, not ours, and we will have to learn to be patient.

But even though this book talks about the importance of the mother-child relationship in terms of development, I want to also put in a plug for not being so invested in outcomes that we turn our children into science projects. Like any flower, tree, or puppy, our children will grow and meet developmental markers if our environment is "good enough." When we get over-focused on getting everything right it has the effect of getting it wrong because we start to mother with our heads and our vanity rather than our hearts. We lose sight of the big picture; we want instant gratification, a fully formed, perfect little person. Immediately, please! No process, no painstaking building. No one would expect to build a successful career in a few months, but many of us want our children to be fully developed faster than they are capable of being. Children should not be pressured or hurried along their developmental paths.

Sound emotional development may have more impact on successful cognitive functioning than all the baby flash cards and mobiles we can fill our child's early worlds with. In fact too much cognitive focus can actually undermine later learning by forcing babies to use parts of their minds that are associated with lower functioning.

What our children need is what they have always needed, love, security, attunement, and support. They need a calm and caring environment to grow up in where people really do get tired and hungry and even fed up. Where they love and get hurt sometimes. Where problems actually happen and everybody lives through them and solves them reasonably well. And children need space and freedom to become, to develop, to fall and get up, to feel bad and work themselves into feeling good again and allow the inventiveness and the elixirs of the childhood mind to work their natural magic. An anxious mother is a liability not an asset, even if the anxiety is "all for the child's good." So as you try to get it right for your child, remember that you are getting it right just by being there, just by caring enough to pick up this book.

Motherhood motivates us to do our best because at some level it's natural to want more for your children than you had. On a material level that may mean a bicycle, a better house, education, or clothes. On a spiritual level it may mean a higher quality of love and connection, greater intimacy, more joy and celebration and less needless pain. This is, after all, how we stumble along and evolve, by seeing a better way and pursuing it in our day to day lives.

We can't imbibe enough vitamins to become fit enough for what motherhood requires. Athletes train their bodies and their minds, but for motherhood you need soul training, and the only place to get it is on the job, because no lab can come close to simulating the experience. Motherhood just grabs you by your insides and doesn't let go and the sooner you can get comfortable with that idea, that it will require more than you ever feel you have to give, the better off you are. That way, when you feel constantly behind the eight ball, you'll feel less inadequate. You'll just expect to feel inadequate and somehow that will help.

Leaning into the loving arms of God, just as our children lean into us, can help us to feel protected, nourished, and carried by "unseen hands." It can lessen our anxiety and maintain our faith that things will work out. Life comes to us in packages of days. "Yesterday is history, tomorrow's a mystery, today is a gift, that's why we call it 'the present.' "

The Miracle of Life

A baby is God's opinion that life should go on.
— Carl Sandburg

When I gave birth to Marina, the earth stood still. Somehow an angel spirit had slid through eons of eternity into the exact spot between my left side and the crook in my arm. "Marina . . . This grace dissolved in place," as T. S. Elliot called it. Until now it felt as if I had been looking for something that I now had a profound sense of having found. A soul that was meant to be here on earth, next to me. This felt not so much like the beginning of my life as the beginning of life itself. This was the place where all the waters meet, the source.

Our children belong ultimately to God, they are leant not given, we do not own them, God does. As Kahlil Gibran says, "we house their bodies but not their spirits." Just as God is within us, he is within them. And just as an acorn will become an oak, a child will grow toward self-awareness and spiritual expansion and expression. And God will find them, even if they get lost. We can pray to God every day of our motherhood to parent side by side with us. We are never alone in this extraordinarily demanding job. We are parenting God's child *with* God, *for* God and *as* God's hands on earth. If our children belong to God, then allowing them to individuate becomes a deeper and much more freeing proposition because we are helping them to individuate not only into themselves but into and toward their God-like natures.

Love and Attention Is Brain Food: Use It or Lose It

The new studies on music and learning stem, in part, from a growing line of research on the development of the human brain. Children are born with 100 billion unconnected or loosely connected neurons, or nerve cells, according to these studies. And each experience, such as seeing a mother's smile or hearing a parent talk, strengthens or forges the links between cells. Pathways in the brain that go unused eventually wither away. Thus, a child's early experiences can help determine what that child will be like in adulthood.

I remember Marina's first cry with crystal clarity. We had rooming in, a very new concept in 1977, which allowed the baby to actually spend her time with the mother instead of lie in a nursery without her, and fathers had unlimited visiting hours. So there she was, lying, wrapped up like a little pastel, perfumed package on my hospital bed. Until this point, Marina had never really uttered much of a peep. She had just opened and closed her big, doe-like eyes as we stared at her thunderstruck. Then suddenly, as if an invisible bell had gone off in her head, she let out a glass-shattering yelp, a thirty-pound sound out of an eight-pound body. I was spellbound, frozen, motionless . . . in shock. I couldn't move and I was painfully aware of that fact. I sat dumbfounded, knowing that I was somehow supposed to know what to do, but having absolutely no idea what it was. Brandt seemed immobilized as well, standing, staring, wondering if this sound was real and if it was coming out of our daughter, who was twenty inches long and had already, in seventy-two hours, brought life as we had known it to a screeching halt. I think I said something like, "Should we call the doctor?" She kept crying. We kept freezing.

Suddenly, as if divinely inspired, Brandt broke his pose and moved toward her. I was flabbergasted, completely mystified at how he had managed to think of doing this brilliant thing. Then he picked her up, and jiggled her and she stopped crying. Thank God I had married some sort of genius.

The Power of the Mother's Voice

Studies have shown that even at birth the child responds positively and specifically to the tones of the human voice, reports Peter Russell in *The Brain Book*. "A high speed film of a newborn baby when slowed down many times and examined frame by frame shows that tiny gestures on the part of the child are synchronized with specific tones and syllables from the parents. Sounds other than the human voice, however, produce no such response. . . . While he is in the womb the child learns the sound of the mother's heartbeat, and after birth the sound of a human heart will have a very soothing effect on the baby." This research also underscores the importance of talking to our babies in order to help them develop language. Children from a fairly normal, not overly enriched environment usually begin talking after the first year of life. By eighteen months they have a vocabulary of about half a dozen words and by two years over two hundred. But a child from birth is sensitized to the parents' voices and attends to them especially. Our babies select our voices out of other sounds or voices to pay rapt attention to.

In her early weeks I was just such a novice. I remember being literally passed out on my bed from exhaustion. I tied a string to Marina's rocking cradle so that I could lie there and pull it, rock her and rest (myself). Every time UPS came to our door with a new baby blanket, I was so enchanted with it that I put it on her. After all they were hers and I wanted her to have them, to feel how many people were thinking about her. Well, she did. After she was a couple of weeks old she broke out in a red rash. Horrified that something foreign was growing on my baby's innocent little body, I flew to the doctor. Eventually, after some questioning, the doctor stared in disbelief to realize that I had seven "light" wool blankets on her in the middle of a hot September. I was so worried about keeping her warm, I had given her a rash.

Emotions Give Texture and Meaning to Our Sensory Input

As we've watched many babies develop over the years, we've come to realize that what have traditionally been described as separate emotional and cognitive (or intellectual) reactions are not so separate after all. In contrast to existing notions, we believe that each time your baby takes in information through his senses, the experience is double-coded as both a physical/cognitive reaction and as an emotional reaction to those sensations. In fact, his emotional reactions may operate like something of a sixth sense, giving each sensory experience texture and meaning.

— Stanley Greenspan, *Building Healthy Minds*

I couldn't figure out how to nurse her. I thought I was somehow supposed to position my body so that she didn't have to move at all. The contorted shapes that I got in were something a gymnast could have bragged about. Eventually it was Brandt who suggested that he'd seen other women just sort of pick the baby up and put her to the breast. I tried it, it worked like a dream. Duh. You just don't know how stupid you're capable of being until you have your first child. I was evidently capable of being really, profoundly dumb. My first few weeks of mothering went along like this, trial and error. Mostly error.

Nothing felt easy and the only times I didn't feel inadequate were when I was sound asleep. I think the first moment when my head got above water was when I looked at Marina and it dawned on me that she was only nine pounds. That just because I was staying at home didn't mean that I had to stay home. I could lift her up and carry her around. I took her straight to Neiman Marcus. We were living outside Chicago at the time and there was a wonderful, indoor world for us to wander around in during the cold winter. I suited us both up and we went out for an adventure. Marina adored it. She loved the car ride, dozed and cooed. She loved her stroller and the light and activity of the atrium. Friendly ladies were constantly stopping to admire her. "That's right, start them young," I remember one lady laughing and saying. I bought a cappuccino and we wheeled around this new world together. I think that is where our friendship began.

Somehow this opened new vistas for me. Marina and I could operate in the world together. Slowly we began to understand each other. Each day I felt stronger and more capable. And very grateful to have pushed through this seemingly insurmountable insecurity into a sense of proficiency. In fact, eventually, motherhood gave me a greater sense of competency than anything I'd ever done before. I was growing in ways I didn't even know were in me, becoming a much more competent, caring, and mature individual. And life wasn't just about me anymore. What a relief. The whole idea of "getting somewhere" took on a new meaning. Just getting out the door felt like such an accomplishment I didn't have room for more. Motherhood helped me to get out of my own way. It freed me. The selflessness and sacrifice that were a necessary part of taking care of Marina, and eventually Alex, actually made me a freer, happier person. One of those paradoxes again, "it is in giving that we receive." I guess that was it. I expanded my emotional container by becoming a mother and now I could take in a lot more of life. I could feel more deeply and fully than I ever had. I could experience joy in a way that was entirely new. And I experienced myself differently, more of myself and a strengthened, better self than I had known before. And love. Love that called to corners of my heart I had forgotten were there. Love that awoke the child in me and brought her back to life. Love that made the world seem soft and giving and tender. Love that brought purpose and meaning into my life.

For the first six months of Marina's life we were almost inseparable. I learned to read her looks and gestures, to anticipate her needs. We got to know each other in a thousand little ways and we developed a quiet rhythm that became both of our lives. When I first had her, I remember feeling completely in the dark as to how to adequately care for her. Whatever instruction booklet everyone else was reading, well, I didn't have it. I felt baffled, inadequate, and more tired than I had ever been before. I also felt that the world had dropped me off and forgotten to pick me up again. I really wasn't sure if I could do this thing called motherhood. I decided to give myself some time, to see if I could push through this feeling into somewhere else. I was "staying at home" with my child, at least much of the time. I felt the walls close in around me. My entire life had been overtaken by something that weighed only eight pounds and had more needs than anyone should be allowed to have. She needed absolutely everything and she needed it NOW.

Motherhood was lonely as well as miraculous, scary as well as comforting, anxiety provoking as well as soothing. But in due course the fear and loneliness subsided and transformed into a kind of knowing, a rhythm and an ever increasing and deepening ability to enter into the moment, the affective or feeling space that existed in the "in between." Though motherhood taught me to make friends with insecurity as a part of me that will always be there in some form or another, it became less undermining as I just accepted it. Eventually, our lives took on a lulling, soothing sort of quality. Seasons became much more important and there were a million holidays throughout the year that I'd almost forgotten about. And time. My life had a different quality of time.

Suiting Up and Showing Up

Suiting up and showing up is something we do every day. We show up for the job of motherhood. I remember when I had Marina. I realized that I could practically spend the day in my nightgown and no one would ever know. Brandt would be at work and Marina was too little to realize what clothes were for what. That's when I decided to take a shower and get dressed at an early, convenient moment; to look nice and take care of myself so that Marina would have a pretty Mommy to model. Every day. I was suiting up and showing up for Marina and my job as her mother. I placed my bet that if Marina thought she was worth my pulling it together every day she would internalize that and do it for herself in her own life. This has proved true for both Marina and Alex. They suit up and show up for their own lives.

The Language of Love

In early stages of development babies learn to experience basic emotions such as pleasure, comfort, and distress. In the months that follow other emotions such as joy, happiness, delight, curiosity, fear, and anger will emerge. "Your 'intimate dialogues' with your child reassure him that his needs can be met and that he can be calmed as well as loved and esteemed."

—See Stanley Greenspan, *Building Healthy Minds*

Don't look over other people's shoulders, look in their eyes. Don't talk at your children. Take their faces in your hands and talk to them. —Leo Buscaglia

Children arrive in the world not knowing exactly how to behave in society and intimate relationships. Though they learn skills of relatedness and behavior extremely rapidly, they do need an environment in which to learn them. They learn about their world through watching their mother's face and interacting with her, through responding to the looks of pleasure, the signals of distress, and the subtle directives and reactions that are constantly crossing their mother's (and father's) face. This language of love is what I remember so well about both Marina's and Alex's early life. I was what we call their "external regulator." I taught Marina and Alex self-regulation by helping them to return from more intense feeling states and maintain balanced ones. I cooed them into serenity when they were agitated, understood their little signals of distress so that I could attend to their needs before their problem got too big, heard their hungry cry, their tired cry, their pick me up and attend right now or let me spill off a little frustration and agitation without over-reacting cry. I knew them; they were my little people to raise. I was their "holding environment." This is how children learn to tolerate, their own strong emotions, to "hold them" first with the parent and eventually on their own. Attending to our children and their emotional needs allows them to experience emotional containment. First they learn to contain their powerful emotions with us, then this ability becomes portable, as they learn to feel, tolerate, and understand their own emotions. The sensory experiences that Marina and Alex and I had, of touching, being held, looking at me and the world, smelling, hearing my voice, feeling my touch are all double coded with emotion. This is what makes intimacy feel like what it feels like. The more senses that are involved in recording an experience, the more the brain remembers it. Mothers who constantly yell at or criticize their children really damage this holding environment and fill it with fear, confusion, and hurt. Mothers who are remote and unavailable make their children feel lost not only to their mothers but to themselves and to the world in general. Mothers who reject rather than embrace their child's natural need to depend raise fragile children.

We teach our children how to regulate their own emotions by how we behave toward them, with them, and around them. Self-regulation is a primary developmental task. A child with a well-regulated limbic system benefits enormously as it is that system that governs such wide-ranging aspects as mood, appetite, sleep cycles, motivation, and motor responses.

Children are great barometers of the emotional atmosphere of a family. They wear it on their faces. They absorb it like little sponges. They act it out. If we want to promote emotional literacy in our children, we need to create a family atmosphere that is easy and relaxed. One in which our children don't have to restrain their emotions, unnaturally. One in which they are free not only to say what they need to say, but to feel what they need to feel. And we need to model emotional regulation ourselves. So many of the problems I treat in adults arise out of a sort of quiet tyranny from their childhoods.

The Portable "Holding Environment"

One of the things parents do for their children is to create what psychologists refer to as a "holding environment," a place of just *being with* our children and their sometimes intense feelings of joy, anger, sadness, or excitement. Of *holding* their inner world *with* them so that they can eventually internalize that ability and hold it within *themselves.* In order to feel safe enough to feel our feelings we need to have a "portable holding environment." We need to have incorporated the "holding" environment we set up with our mothers, fathers, families, and early environment into ourselves and walk around with it.

How Emotion Lives In and Travels through the Body

"The body is the unconscious mind," says Georgetown University research professor Candace Pert in *Molecules of Emotion.* Until recently, emotions have been considered to be location-specific, associated with emotional centers in the brain such as the amygdala, hippocampus, and hypothalamus. While these are, in fact, emotional centers, other types of centers are strewn throughout our bodies. Emotions travel through our bodies and bind to small receptors on the outside of cells, much like tiny satellite dishes. There are many locations throughout the body where high concentrations of almost every neuropeptide receptor exist. Nuclei serve as the source of most brain-to-body and body-to-brain hookups. Nuclei are peptide-containing groups of neuronal cell bodies in the brain.

Emotional information travels on neuropeptides and is able to bind to its receptor cells through the binding substance of ligands. The information is sorted through the differentiation of receptors. That is, certain information binds to certain receptors. So our emotions are constantly being processed by our bodies. The brain and body are exquisitely intertwined systems that are constantly interacting with the environment. All five senses are connected to this system and feed information that determines our unique response to anything from petting a soft rabbit to being slapped. The more senses involved in an experience, the more the brain remembers it. The *smell* and *taste* of Grandma's cooking — as well as her gentle *touch*, familiar *voice*, and the *sight* of her standing at the stove — all engrave themselves onto our memory systems, along with the feelings associated with them because every sense is involved. The same is true in the case of painful experiences.

Darwin felt this system was highly conserved throughout evolution because emotions were so critical to our survival. The cavewoman who got scared when she sensed danger from a potentially threatening animal and removed her baby, whom she wanted to protect and nurture into adulthood, was the one who survived and kept our species alive. She is the DNA strain that led to us.   — Tian Dayton, *The Magic of Forgiveness*

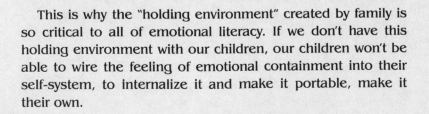

This is why the "holding environment" created by family is so critical to all of emotional literacy. If we don't have this holding environment with our children, our children won't be able to wire the feeling of emotional containment into their self-system, to internalize it and make it portable, make it their own.

The Mother-Child Bond: Where It All Begins

Perhaps a child who is fussed over gets a feeling of destiny, he thinks that he is in the world for something important and it gives him drive and confidence.

— Benjamin Spock, M.D.

Most moms hopefully learn to respond to their child's various signals in a reasonable and attuned fashion. We learn which cries are tired cries, frustration unwinding at the end of the day, and which ones are distress signals that need immediate attention. Most moms, though overwhelmed by never having a moment to themselves to brush their hair or blow their nose, understand that their little ones are just trying to get what they need to make it to the next day. Though there is frustration inevitably on both sides, a loving, secure attachment can make it a constructive sort of frustration. One in which the child can learn that she won't die of her own neediness and she can postpone gratification for increasing bits of time without falling apart. And the mother learns that she can stretch her capacity for giving along with her ability to multitask on all levels emotionally, psychologically, and physically. She can respond to varying degrees depending on the level of response required. This is a great opportunity for both mother and child to learn self-regulation and self-soothing. The mom learns not to lose it just because her child is losing it and the child gets wooed back to center by a mom who can hang onto her own center. Both benefit and strengthen a sort of ability to keep their cool under crisis and to calm themselves when agitated.

Our children also learn to tolerate increasing amounts of time away from us; then they return to our knee, to their safe base. First maybe it's a couple of feet, then a whole play yard and gradually a school day. Current research studies refer to the child's checking on the availability and attentiveness of the caregiver in a sort of permanent monitoring activity.

The healthy relationship of a small child with her mother lies in keeping a balance between these two systems of connection,

movement toward and away. This is referred to, in the lit-
erature, as developing a "secure base." There are several
categories of attachment; the most straightforward are *secure*
and *insecure* attachment. Children who are securely attached
generally tend to develop more positively across a range of in-
dicators than children who are insecurely attached. They feel
the mother is a base from which they can explore the world.
They feel assured that they can move out into the world and
return for comfort, reassurance, and care when they need to.
When there is an insecure attachment they also return but they
don't receive the reassurance that they seek and need. This
leaves a definite void. In my own clients, I see that a sort of
psychic searching gets set up, if the mothers or fathers are too
unavailable. This psychic searching, in my experience, affects
development because part of the child's energy gets devoted
to constantly seeking out what they are looking for, trying to
establish a secure base, rather than simply exploring the world
from their already existing one. On the other hand, we mothers
can be too available, insinuating ourselves into each and every
moment of a child's life, which the child can experience as controlling and intrusive. A secure base is just that, a center from
which the child can move in ever increasing concentric circles
outward, with the assuredness that home plate is available to
him when and as he needs it. It is a back and forth movement.

Children who develop this secure base at a young age tend
to be more independent. The secure attachment boosts their
self-esteem and helps them to be self-reliant and enjoy their
relationships with peers. They also tend to do better in school,
especially in mathematics. Their secure bond affects both at-
tendance and achievement. If you think about it, the whole idea
of accountability implies that there is someone who cares at the
other end and that we are, in some way, accountable to them.
Why would a child who feels they don't matter to anyone feel accountable to attend school? By the time a child gets to school
age, these patterns are already well in place. Motherhood is
not only about what we do *to* the child but who we are *with*
the child; who the child learns to be *in relationship*. Because

this learning how to connect, disconnect, and reconnect, this learning how to be "in relationship or in rapport" with another person, is what we take into all of our relationships.

Mothering Styles

Daniel Stern has outlined three common patterns of mothering that he has observed in his research. They are *enmeshed*, *disengaged*, and *modulated*.

In the *enmeshed* style mothers tend to have fuzzy boundaries. The mother is not sure where she leaves off and the child begins. She is not good at separating her own inner world from that of her child, there is lots of overlap, the kind of overlap that confuses and fuses things, not the kind that is a natural part of the co-state of intimacy.

In the *disengaged* style, the mother doesn't fully engage in her new role as mother. She may be somewhat intellectual and aloof. Or more likely she engages and then disengages and doesn't really carry her child around inside of her the way a more engaged mother does. She leaves them psychically behind, so to speak.

The third style is *modulated*. In this style, the mother's mind oscillates back and forth between her child and herself in a sort of evenhanded way. She has awareness of her own self and of the self of the child. She is able to maintain a sense of self and allow her child to do the same. She can balance her own needs with those of her child in her own mind, recognizing that an awareness of both is important.

It is impossible to talk about emotional literacy without talking about this bond, because without the bond emotions are meaningless. This is where we learn about emotion. This is where the experience is born. Only once it exists can we name it. Without the experience of connection, there is no place to attach the word "love" or "caring." If you can't see the color green, the name has nowhere to stick; if you have no direct experience of love, hurt, yearning and satisfaction, anger, or pleasure, then there is no way to attach the name to a feeling. No emotional literacy.

Attachment Styles

Through observing the behavior of mothers and children Mary Ainsworth, a psychologist who worked at Johns Hopkins, explored not only if children attach, but how they attach. She was able, with her research, to delineate three categories of attachment: *secure, insecure/avoidant,* and *ambivalent/preoccupied*. Basically, she set up a room with toys in which mother and child played and grew comfortable. A typical *securely* attached child will play happily with the toys while Mom is in the room. When Mom leaves the room, the securely attached child will show signs of missing her and cry when left alone. Then when they reunite, the child tugs on her leg to be picked up and snuggle into her body. The *insecure/avoidant* child shows no distress at her leaving, continuing to play with the toys. When she returns, there is no warm reunion; the child may ignore, turn away from, or stiffen at Mom's approach. The *ambivalent/preoccupied* child behaves differently from both other groups. She does not engage in play with the toys, showing lack of interest, or being fretful and clingy with Mom. This child shows great distress when Mom leaves.

The mother's behavior varied in the development of each attachment style. Ainsworth found that in the first group of children, the mothers had been attuned and sensitive to the children's needs, responding promptly when they expressed need and having warm physical contact. In the avoidant group, though things seemed to run smoothly, the babies' bodies told a different story: their heart rates went high during separations; they seemed angry at their mothers and were distressed at even minor separations. Mothers in this group often said they didn't like being touched and seemed to rebuke their children's attempts at connecting.

In the third group, though the mothers reported feeling love for their children and invested in their welfare, they were unattuned caretakers who lacked good mothering skills. They appeared to give their children enough love to understand the feeling but not enough to feel secure.

— Tian Dayton, *The Magic of Forgiveness*

𝒜 New Center to the Universe
The day the earth stood still

Stay, stay home my heart and rest;
Home-keeping hearts are happiest.
— Henry Wadsworth Longfellow

Sitting bolt upright on the floor illuminated by a shaft of light as celestial and otherworldly as her little being — everything I wanted was right in this house. What in the outside world could compete with what was here in the corner of my living room? Sure I was self-conscious not to be working — even more self-conscious not to care — but how could I explain to anyone (including me) that everything fun and exciting, everything that mattered was right at my fingertips and I just couldn't miss it? Marina opened doors inside my soul, she called to something deep inside of me — something eternal and God-like . . . something that put me in touch with the core of creation. We shared a rare moment carved out of time and I would let the world pass by until we could enter it together. These moments were too precious to lose. I don't mean to imply that it was easy. It wasn't. I remember at the time wanting to write a book called "Motherhood, the Toughest Job You'll Ever Love." Nothing I had done to this point had prepared me for how hard it was to be a mother, to feel both marginalized from the rest of the world and as if I had finally met my own soul. Nothing had prepared me for the endlessness of the work, the overwhelming feeling of ineptitude, or the mind-bending fears of something bad happening to this little girl. And nothing prepared me for the love. The transformation of my spirit.

The Love Loop

At approximately eight weeks, a miraculous thing occurs — your baby's vision improves and for the first time, she can fully see you and can make direct eye contact. These beginning visual experiences of your baby play an important role in social and emotional development. "In particular, the mother's emotionally expressive face is, by far, the most potent visual stimulus in the infant's environment," points out UCLA's Alan Schore, "and the child's intense interest in her face, especially in her eyes, leads him/her to track it in space to engage in periods of intense mutual gaze." The result is that endorphin levels rise in the baby's brain (and the mother's), causing pleasurable feelings of joy and excitement. But the key is for this joy to be interactive.

We now know that the baby's participation is crucial to creating a solid attachment bond. The loving gaze of parents to child is reciprocated by the baby with a loving gaze back to the parents, causing all their endorphin levels to rise, thus completing a closed emotional circuit, a sort of "love loop." Now parent and baby are truly in a dynamic, interactive system. "In essence, we are talking less about what the mother is doing *to* the baby and more about how the mother is being *with* the baby and how the baby is learning to be with the mother," says Schore. The final aspect of this developing interactive system between mother and child is the mother's development of an "emotional synchronization" with her child. Schore defines this as the mother's ability to tune into the baby's internal states and respond accordingly.

It was this mingling of spirits that I called motherhood. We raised each other, Marina and I, entering into each other's worlds like sisters in spirit seeking knowledge and adventure. All the while I was caring for her, she was nourishing me. Be more than you were was the gentle call I felt from her, see me and in seeing me see more of you. Ahh, eeeeekkk, aahhaaa — her experiments in sound — I doubled her sounds. Yes you are here, my little love, someone sees you, someone hears you, you are alive and I am your mother.

This is where emotional literacy began. This psychological and emotional connection was the foundation for all of her emotional learning. Together we could figure out what hurt, what felt good, what feeling matched up with the word "happy" and what hurt could be best explained by the word "owie" or "sad." Some feelings, and this is important to know, are named mommy, because when children are small and vulnerable and dependent their mommies are the whole world. When mommy sees and understands, the world sees and understands and when mommy turns away the world goes dark.

Developing a strong bond is number one in raising an emotionally intelligent child. Emotional information flows back and forth through this bond from mother to child and child to mother. Dependency needs are adequately met because this bond allows the mother to attune to the needs of the child and the child to attune to the needs of the mother and for both to adapt empathically. The mother senses what is going on in the inner world of her child and responds accordingly and the child senses what is going on in the inner world of her mother and also adapts. That's why we can't hide from our children and why we owe it to them to clear out our emotional baggage so that they don't have to live with it in their emotional world. Early in development the child doesn't really know the difference between herself and her mother. She lives in an undifferentiated world, a sort of we-ness, joined at the heart, so to speak. How her mother sees her becomes how she sees herself. And how her mother holds her becomes, in an emotional sense, how she "holds" herself.

The Subtle and Significant Communication between Mother and Infant

Pregnancy and birth form the beginning of an on-going inter-action between mother and infant which involves intersubjective communication (Stern 1985) and that evolves with the growing and interrelated perceptual, cognitive and motor capacities of the infant.

The early post-natal development of most non-human primates occurs in an environment formed in large part by the mother's body. Closely attached to her, the infant must become intimately acquainted with the tactual, kinesthetic, auditory, visual, and olfactory stimuli that she provides. To some of these stimuli he responds as soon as he is born. As he develops further, his mother's body is his first toy, and many of his waking hours are spent in its exploration. In addition, the manner in which the mother holds the baby makes it easier for the baby to learn her features. She likes to look into her baby's face, and tries to get the baby to look at her. Being held and rocked may not only soothe a crying baby, but also alert it, and when the infant is at the breast, its mother's face is at about the distance at which it can focus most clearly. (Let us remember infants are myopic at birth and that their visual focal distance is barely 25–30 cms.)

. . . There is evidence that infants exposed to the sound of the human heartbeat gain weight better than do infants not so exposed: the tendency of parents to carry babies against the left breast rather than the right may be related to this. One of the most outstanding communication features deployed by mammals in general and humans in particular are distress signals. Human infants' cries adopt different patterns: in hunger, it progresses from an arrhythimical low-intensity cry to a louder and rhythmical form; an angry cry, somewhat similar in form but with the components of the sequence differently emphasized; and a pain cry, with a sudden urgency.

—Daniel Goleman, *How Emotions Matter for Health*

Slowly the child discovers that she has her own body that is different from her mother's. Though her mother still feels like an extension of her, the child begins to feel some sense of autonomy. It is a much longer and more complicated individuation process to understand that her mind and emotions are also separate. And truthfully, because we incorporate our mothers' emotions and thoughts and often experience them as our own, and because our constant interaction with our mothers actually gets imprinted in the neural wiring throughout our systems, part of separation is an illusion. I prefer words like self-defining and individuation. We are really like tapestries or mosaics, threads and pieces from all throughout our lives woven through us, pieced together to create an ever changing, constantly evolving whole. Making peace with the mother who lives inside us brings a sort of integration and inner calm because, like it or not, she is there anyway.

Are You in There, Little Alexander?

When I was carrying Alex, I used to talk to him every day (in my mind). "You're going to surprise everyone, you're going to burst forward, be born easily and quickly at a convenient time of day." I got to know him by looking at my face in the mirror while he was inside of me. I adored him. I respected his spirit, strength, and zest for life as it coursed through my own being.

And he was born just as we'd agreed. Marina and I had spent the morning making play dough and rolling it out and cutting it into shapes. Then Brandt's sister Lucy called. Lucy is a vet and she began telling us about a calf that she had birthed. As I was listening my whole mind felt for that mother cow. I felt like I was her lying in the hay straining to give birth.

Very self-consciously I said that I thought I might be going into labor. Brandt thought I was just really going over the top. The second time I said it, Lucy told us to get off the phone and call the doctor — that was around twelve-thirty. I showered, called my friend who had planned to take Marina, and we casually drove to the hospital. We ran into a couple of people we knew and chatted — I still felt fine even though I was having pretty regular contractions. Then I knew — something was going on. Alex was born an hour and a half later. I felt like an Amazon woman. Like, true to my Greek roots, I could have given birth under a tree. Alex and I just worked together and did it — I still give him a lot of the credit, he just somehow figured it all out. He and I spent our first week on a king-size bed that felt like it was a cloud in heaven, floating, defying gravity, a world of four of us. Brandt and Marina were home and on the bed a lot of the time, too. Time carved out of time.

I really think the communication bond started with Alex and I before birth and, as you might imagine, we have always understood each other intuitively. I remember once I was choking on something and six people at least were trying to help me but the voice that I could hear and use in that terrifying moment was his. "Don't panic mom, hold onto yourself, you're ok, you're just scared, calm down and breathe." I stopped choking immediately. Something in that voice.... Something in that emotional bond. He has depth and he has slowly learned how to live with the blessing and the burden of seeing deeply and feeling fully. He's hysterically funny; he translates potentially awkward situations into humor that throws everything up in the air and gets it to fall back down again somehow in a better place. And he has learned to witness his own emotions, sit with them, feel them, and translate them into words.

When Marina was a baby I used to put her in a snuggly and she would lean against my chest as I cleaned the house or we did errands together. She loved and was comforted by this position and so was I. We spent countless hours just like this, and after Alex was born I felt guilty for not being able to give him this kind of one-to-one attention and looked forward to finding a few moments when I could. I remember taking him, just the two us, to do some errands. I tucked him carefully into the snuggly. He was a little fussy, but I assumed as soon as he felt our rhythm walking he would, of course, calm down. As I approached the store I felt little fists pounding on my chest, fists that I didn't realize my two-month-old even had. "Shhhh, sweetheart, Mommy's right here, we're going to have such a sweet time together. . . . " Next, as we entered the tiny antique store I had saved for our special errand he began to shift his weight from side to side as he continued to pound his baby fists much harder than I would have thought possible into my collar bone. "Ali, Darling, what izzzz it? What are you trying to tell me, Koukla?" Duh. I had been so excited to repeat the precious moments I remembered having with Marina in a snuggly, that I just assumed it would be the same with Alex. I didn't get rule number one of motherhood. Each child is different; adapt your bonding style to your child's.

I ran for the door of the antique store just as Alex threw the full weight of his tiny but strong and determined little body so hard that I almost knocked over an entire, three-tiered table of glass and china chachkas. I can still see the table perfectly clearly in my mind and even recall the atmosphere of the store, the smell of dust and the sight of small glass bottles. That table was almost a goner. Woops, wrong approach. Better back up and try again. In a desperate attempt to figure out a way to use this snuggly (all the rage with the modern mom at that time), I put Alex in facing out, though I really felt I was do-ing it all wrong and people would look at me like some sort of insensitive mother who hung my son like a necklace on my chest.

He loved it. He laughed and smiled up a storm, stared at everyone who passed, turned his head all over the place to track people's movement, and generally let me know by his vastly more agreeable behavior that I had gotten it right *for him* . . . finally. I learned to like it too and to recognize that my children, like snowflakes, were each their own unique design.

Each Day a New Beginning
Let the world be their play pen

Your children are not your children, they are the sons and daughters of life's longing for itself. They come through you, but not from you. And though they are with you, yet they belong not to you.
— Kahlil Gibran

I understood from my training both as a Montessori teacher and as a psychologist that my children needed to use me and use their home as classroom for learning. What they needed to learn couldn't wait. Their play pen was basically a child-proofed, supervised house.

We led a child-size life as much as possible. A life that could adjust to their rhythm and needs. I came to enjoy the soothing world of motherhood and naturally adapted to their schedule. Motherhood was so exhausting that I flopped into bed practically when they did. Though Brandt and I didn't have the time we needed together and had to fix that as the children grew older, I felt a sense of romance develop around being a tender little family that was utterly enveloping. And it fulfilled a dream of motherhood and family that was part of my biology. It called to the little girl in me who felt safe in my own home and also gave me an opportunity to repair the part of me that felt shattered by my loss of a feeling of safety from my parent's divorce, Dad's alcoholism, and Mom's deep sorrow. I reintegrated lost or frozen parts of me. As I made Marina and Alex a safe, secure little home to grow up in, I made one for me, too. Emotional repair.

In my efforts to make our home a classroom I began with me. I nursed, held, cuddled, cooed, rolled around with, massaged, and otherwise engaged both Marina and Alex as much as possible. We played and plopped around. I tried to make whatever we did pleasurable or adventurous. If I was changing them I goofed around with them and admired their enormous

42

efforts at elimination. If they hurt, I winced. If they giggled, I giggled. I tried to stay engaged in their little world so that I would naturally know where they were and what they needed.

I let the children explore freely so that their home became a sensorial experience. They rolled on rugs and floors, touched their way from one end of the house to the other. We played classical music, which they seemed to love. I let them touch everything, including every part of my face, which seemed to captivate them.

I used eating to encourage hand-eye coordination by cutting their food into little pieces and letting them feed themselves. When I cooked or cleaned up in the kitchen, they loved to sit in the sink with a few inches of water and a measuring cup, bubbles, and a sponge. It kept them happy, appealed to their senses, and let me keep an eye on them while I got things done. As they got older, I let them help me prepare. They had plastic knives, a little cutting board, a small rolling pin, iddy-biddy bowls with wire whips and spoons. There was always some part of dinner preparation that could be broken down to child size if they wanted to help in the kitchen.

Rather than banish them to cordoned-off corners, I tried to incorporate them into what I was doing so that they could learn, grow, and feel connected. It's not that I didn't use all the ordinary stuff to keep my kids occupied, but I tried to keep those things at a sort of minimum. Part of keeping children safe is to help them to learn how to function in the real world and keep themselves safe. Life was our classroom and I was the catalyst between them and their learning environment. In most rooms we had cupboards or drawers that the children could operate and things they could take out and examine, look at carefully, play with or explore. My mother always kept a toy drawer in the kitchen and I still remember sitting by it and playing with what was in it. She also let me have little projects all over the place. The only rules I remember were to keep each one more or less together and to try to finish things I had started. Those requests sort of floated above my head and gave me a bit of structure, but they were never oppressive. Basically I felt free to pursue my own, independent little path as long as I didn't cause trouble. J. L. Moreno, the father of psychodrama, cautioned not to fill the child's world with too many "robot"-like, mechanical things that didn't provide natural, human contact and feedback. He felt that children should engage in spontaneous interaction with people who said ouch if you hit them and smiled when you made them happy or with animals that were alive and real. Montessori emphasized letting the children have supervised contact with some non-plastic things that broke if you dropped them so that children would learn to respect beauty. Marina could pick up a piece of Steuben glass, admire it, and return it to its shelf unharmed. I kept our Steuben on the bottom shelf so that she could enjoy it.

When Alex came along, I was so used to this that I watched with no particular amazement as he picked up the glass goose with the long neck, turned it over in his little hands, and smiled admiringly at its delicate form. Luckily, I made a magnificent save when, with his little hand around the neck, he drew it back over his shoulder and was about to explore whether or not the glass goose shattered when he threw it. I grabbed it just in time. I promptly got the message that each child is unique and moved the Steuben to a shelf well out of his reach. Alex needed to test the world in different ways from Marina. He needed to rub up directly against it, climb each and every part of it, and throw a lot of it to see what would happen to it if he did. Alex learned eventually that things really do break and he needed to be careful. He translated this sense of being careful into his play and could be very active but still sensitive to and aware of physical danger. He became sure footed.

I really felt that motherhood made amazing physical demands. Not only because I never sat down and also developed biceps I didn't know were possible from constantly lifting and carrying my kids and literally everything else in their world, but because there was so much, well, body contact. I was their jungle gym, their live food dispenser, their constant servant, their physical object to punch, suck, cuddle, climb, roll on, pinch, lick—you name it. It felt like no part of me was left untouched or unexamined. Motherhood "felt" wonderful to me (on most days) and I hope that childhood "felt" wonderful to them. We licked batter, ate peanut butter off a spoon, slurped dripping ice cream cones, rolled down grassy hills, burrowed into covers, pillows, and each other, and generally filled our senses to the brim with the physical as well as the emotional pleasures of life.

The Nuts and Bolts of Developing Emotional Intelligence and Literacy
Stanley Greenspan's Six Developmental Levels of the Mind

The following is a progression of development outlined by Stanley Greenspan, M.D., author of *Building Healthy Minds*. It describes how a baby translates the raw data she gathers from her senses and inner feelings into images. She uses these images to create personal meaning and in communication with others. We can think of them as the mind's deepest structural components, which support all later development. They are the foundations of sound emotional development.

1. **Self-regulation:** Self-regulation is a primary developmental task that allows the child to regulate herself or himself *emotionally* and *physically*. Regulating the self involves learning to *organize sensations and the body's responses*. From a jumble of sounds, sights, smells, and tactile feelings, patterns begin to emerge. Sounds become rhythms, sights become recognizable images. And a child's growing ability to control body movements make it possible to cuddle, to follow an object, or to stand up in his mother's lap. *Physical and emotional self-regulation are at the core of healthy functioning on all levels.*

2. **Engagement:** Engagement represents the *beginning of building the capacity for relationships*. It begins with the child's

emotional registering and awareness of a fellow being's presence. Through using her capacity for calm attention, the baby now notices the tones, expressions, and actions of the people close to her. Before long she reacts to them with pleasure and starts building intimate relationships with those who love her. Without some degree of adoring wooing by at least one adult who cares about her, a child may never know the powerful intoxication of human closeness, never see other people as full human beings like herself, capable of feeling what she feels. This is the reason that, in studies of why some children develop the resilience that allows them to thrive in adverse circumstances that often sink others, the single most important buffering and sustaining factor in that child's life is at least *one bonded relationship*.

3. **Intentionality:** The ability to connect with at least one other person leads to intentionality — a willed exchange of signals and responses. Children who have successfully completed the passage into deep engagement gradually come to perceive that the actions passing between themselves and others are part of a two-way exchange. There is such a thing as *intent* in the world — a smile leads to a smile; outstretched arms lead to being picked up; and so on.

4. **Purpose and Interaction:** Once a child connects sensation and emotion to intentional action, more complex, presymbolic communication equips him to find his way in the world of social interaction. He can now distinguish facial expressions and body gestures, and discriminate among basic emotions, distinguishing those meaning safety and comfort from those meaning danger. Life's most essential, emotional themes are identified and patterns of dealing with them formed.

5. **Images, Ideas, and Symbols:** This is the stage of true symbolic expression. The child begins to deal not only with behavior but with ideas. She begins to understand that one thing can stand for another, that an image of something can represent the thing itself. This realization allows her to create

an inner picture of her world. Moreover, these symbols (i.e., mental pictures, gestures, feeling states, or words) can represent not only her own intentions, wishes, and feelings but those of other people as well.

6. **Emotional thinking:** Experience now can be linked into sequences of inner images that allow a child to consider actions before carrying them out. *Words* and then *ideas* can link up to *emotions:* "I am sad because it's raining and I want to play outside." Time becomes more comprehensible, separated into past, present, and future. These abilities together make up basic personality or ego functions. They include *reality testing, impulse control,* and *ability to see connections among many different feelings and ideas.*

Through practicing these principles *nature* and *nurture can interact toward sound emotional development.* Without this structure the mind cannot function coherently, but functions only in a fragmented, jumbled fashion. Greenspan uses what he refers to as "floor time" to nurture all six levels of intelligence and emotional health at the same time. He says that "During this time you'll be getting down on your child's level, joining him in his world and on his terms. You'll be encouraging him to be the boss of all the drama that unfolds, and will follow his lead as an ever-willing sidekick. . . . When you are playing eye-to-eye with your child, you will generate a sense of equality that encourages him to engage with you." Children emerge from this kind of play with greater self-confidence and self-awareness. This one-to-one, intentional time with a caring, relaxed, and attuned adult is worth its weight in gold to a child. It is an investment in their inner world from which they will draw interest all through their lives.

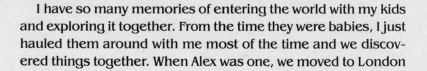

I have so many memories of entering the world with my kids and exploring it together. From the time they were babies, I just hauled them around with me most of the time and we discovered things together. When Alex was one, we moved to London for a couple of years. Living around four blocks from Holland Park completely saved our lives. Our routine was to take a slow (very slow, unbelievably slow, in fact) walk to the park and play with the other children. Marina was in nursery school so Alex and I had the morning to do what he wanted to, which was seldom what Marina wanted to do. I remembered from my Montessori training to walk at the child's pace, which meant that it took us around forty-five minutes to go four blocks. But for Alex, new to the world, there was more adventure in that little walk than in all the climbing toys he could have. There was the spigot that stood out from the wall, the curbs . . . getting up and down them carefully, cracks in the side walk, window boxes, stores, cars, trucks, and wonderful smells pouring out of the café on the corner where we sometimes had tea and scones — hot with clotted cream and jam (an adventure unto itself). Occasionally a friendly dog would come into our world to meet and pet and smell and hear. The world was full of so many sights and sounds just in those few blocks. No "enriched environment" could possibly compete with these little forays into the world that surrounded us.

Floor Time —
Finding Where the Soul Is Hidden

There is a scene from *Baby Boom* with Diane Keaton that always brings tears to my eyes. She has just come back from her big success in New York, the success she thought she'd been waiting for all her life. As she enters her farmhouse living room, she stops in her tracks at the sight of her daughter, sitting on her blanket with sunlight streaming in through the window, bathing her little girl in the kind of light appropriate for a heavenly being. "What'dya do, what'dya do?" she asks gazing, transfixed and transformed at the sight of her whole world sitting peacefully on a patchwork quilt.

I have countless memories of Marina just like this. In the countryside where we were living, sitting, wrapped in peacefulness, on her yellow and white blanket. My world, by contrast, felt dull and worn, but her little world was filled with a kind of luminescence and aliveness that moved my whole being. It was easy to leave the cares of the world behind as I entered Marina's quiet. Time stood still as I felt the touch of two, soft little hands cupping my cheeks. "Hello, Mommy, I missed you." "Hello, Marina, I missed you just as much."

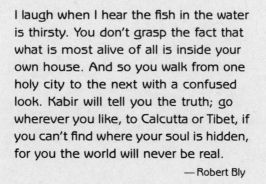

> I laugh when I hear the fish in the water
> is thirsty. You don't grasp the fact that
> what is most alive of all is inside your
> own house. And so you walk from one
> holy city to the next with a confused
> look. Kabir will tell you the truth; go
> wherever you like, to Calcutta or Tibet, if
> you can't find where your soul is hidden,
> for you the world will never be real.
>
> —Robert Bly

There was a kind of magic that took me over when I let myself enter Marina's and Alex's worlds. Some of it was simply the magic of love. The stirring in my heart of something deep and far away, God calling me toward him through his little people. A lot of these memories are centered around sitting on the floor. Sitting on Marina's blanket, talking to her, touching, cooing, letting her touch me, learn me, and have me at her fingertips. Letting her guide the action as I followed her into her private world of caresses, sounds, and movements. What makes you tick, little one? What is in your sweet little mind? What delights you, frightens you, sends you into peals of laughter or brings tears to your eyes? What makes your lower lip go out like that and your eyes stare at me till I notice your sign for "something's not right, pay attention to me"?

Basically I remember spending the first few years of my children's lives on the floor. That's where they were so that's where I wound up half the time. When they learned to sit up and pass things from hand to hand at around six months I wanted to let off fireworks it felt like such a milestone and relief. Floor time is intimate, one-to-one time. Time when we can enter the world of our child, follow her lead, and help her to extend and elaborate on the direction in which she wishes to go.

The Basic Ideas Involved in "Floor Time"
From the work of Stanley Greenspan

Observation

As we listen to and watch our child we are observing. Facial expressions, tone of voice, gestures, body posture, and words (or lack of words) are all-important clues that help us determine how to approach our child. Is his behavior relaxed or outgoing? Is he or she withdrawn or uncommunicative or content and interactive?

Approach — Open Circles of Communication

As we tune into "where our child is" we can open the circle of communication by acknowledging our child's emotional tone, then elaborating and building on whatever interests her or him at the moment.

Follow the Child's Lead

Following a child's lead simply means being a supportive play partner who is an "assistant" to the child and allows the child to set the tone, direct the action, and create personal dramas. This enhances the child's self-esteem and ability to be assertive, and gives the child a feeling that *"I can have an impact on the world."* As you support your child's play, he benefits from experiencing a sense of warmth, connectedness, and being understood.

Extend and Expand Play

As you follow your child's lead, extending and expanding your child's play themes, he will feel your interest and be strengthened and emboldened by it. This involves making supportive comments about your child's play without being intrusive. This helps your child express his own ideas and defines the direction of the drama or interactive play. Next, asking questions to stimulate creative thinking can keep the drama evolving, while helping the child clarify the emotional themes involved, e.g.: suppose your child is playing out super-hero themes: Rather than ask about the villains critically, *Why are those people so awful?* You may respond empathetically, *What does that "person" want? What are they doing now?*

The Child Closes the Circle of Communications

You open the circle of communication when you approach your child, then your child closes the circle when she builds on your comments and gestures with comments and gestures of her own. One circle flows into another, and many circles may be opened and closed in quick succession as you and your child interact. By building on each other's ideas and gestures, your child begins to appreciate and understand the value of two-way communication.

Interestingly, psychodrama, the role-playing method I use in my practice, follows the exact same principles as floor time. In psychodrama, we follow the lead of the protagonist or the person telling their story, just as the parent follows the child's lead in floor time. We help them to fill out or elaborate on the direction in which they wish to go, to explore their drama, the inner world that they are bringing to the outside. We assist them in their investigation, in playing out their drama and bringing it to a comfortable sense of closure. Intuitively this healing method recreates the kind of early environment that encourages emotional growth. Children need this approach so that they can build sound emotional foundations and adults need it to repair damaged ones.

Alex's floor time was very active. Full of movement. He was constantly leaning over, scooting, trying to crawl or pulling himself up on anything he could reach. As he grew a little older his time was often spent running or riding or climbing or throwing. Running everywhere, riding anything, climbing everything, and throwing any item he could wrap his hand around to test its velocity. His favorite thing to do on the floor was fantasy play. As a toddler he could spend hours on his stomach or knees, crawling around with one hand holding a horse or a tiger or a person and creating endless scenarios in which he supplied sound and dialogue. His imaginary play allowed him to operate in a universe of his choosing, to transcend the boundaries of ordinary life, to enter a world where he was in charge and could correct, through fantasy, the humiliating power imbalances of his day-to-day life or explore the intriguing world beyond his fingertips. His growing ability to see and decode patterns was ever present in the way in which he organized the characters in his private realm, where he practiced all of the skills and types of relating that he internalized throughout his day. "You be the teacher and I'll be the student," he would say as he played out scenarios that had taught, inspired, or hurt him. Then he might reverse roles and empower himself to admonish, comfort, or teach: "Now you be the student and I'll be the teacher." And he would proceed, "Now, you have to sit still for a minute and I'll read you a story, isn't this fun? No, no, no, stop that, that's good. Okay, let's play with the blocks now." His mind would skip around to various scenes of the day and he could comfort himself after being reprimanded, encourage himself to try something, or congratulate himself for a job well done; all in his private little theater. The one where all the characters represented him in some way, his real life, his fantasy life, his inner and outer world. There he was, zooming through space, growling at an adversary, kissing a baby, cooing, cawing, laughing and pretending to cry in the way that children do when they use their toy world as a stage on which to play out their lives. He used his little floor theater to resolve small hurts of the day, bringing them to comfortable closure, exacting revenge on an unsuspecting adversary by whom he felt wronged, and being a special cheerleader to the part of him that wanted the recognition and encouragement that we all crave. He also used it to ignite his imagination, leaping from world to world like a little water sprite skipping from land to stone and back to land again. He met his marks with the agility of a dancer and the accuracy of an archer.

And when I joined in, it was just together time. No rules, no authority, no pulling rank. We were explorers together, co-creating "Planet Alex," an Alex-friendly-ambience in which he could take the lead and I could follow. A respite from our daily routine in which he was always the small one and I essentially had the power. In our "private world of Counterpane," he was the captain of his ship and I was the first mate, he navigated, I attended, as the wind filled out our waiting sails and we charged through the waves together, bumping, often nearly capsizing, then basking in the sunlight of our accomplishments. He was in charge and I was his faithful, willing sidekick.

Floor time is not always on the floor. It is a philosophy, a way of relating that can happen at any age and in any place. When Marina and Alex became teenagers, the way of intimate, attuned relating that we had begun on the floor extended into hang-out time, together time, talking time. And as adults it has become a rich and genuine exchange; sometimes playful and silly, sometimes serious and exploratory, sometimes just doing things together.

Play Is the Work of Childhood

The most effective education is that a child should play among lovely things.
— Plato

Montessori felt that children have "work" or "play" periods that grow deeper if they are allowed to pursue them without unnecessary interruption. I witnessed this with both of the children. Their ability to concentrate, to focus, to become purposeful and attending, and to regulate their moods grew if they were allowed to pursue their little paths of play without much interference or unneeded direction. What they seemed to need, in addition to the type of interaction described in "floor time" was what Montessori referred to as the "prepared environment" and a calm, pleasant, and predictable world. If I was just around, I could help to create that simply by being in the moment and more or less sharing the same world together. Sometimes they needed me to drop everything and attend, to be with them in their world. And sometimes they just needed space, time, and the knowledge that I was available if and when needed.

Alex's deep play was fantasy oriented. He would go into his room and get intensely involved in what we might call his "scenarios." He might be playing with his mountain or his castle and his soldiers, his action figures and little people. There would often be animals and vehicles of some sort. He would enter a sort of trance-like state in which time would clearly disappear, a "flow state" in which he and his activity became one. If I interrupted this it was clearly jarring, as if I had gone into a coughing fit just in the middle of a beautiful concert. His room seemed to be filled with a kind of quiet, vibrating light. A meditative state. He made sweet little sounds to accompany his scenarios. And he didn't like to be interrupted. He was deep at play and if I allowed him to enter in and out of it as he wished, his play periods became progressively and subsequently deeper and longer. He would emerge from them centered, calm, and happy.

Marina seemed to enter her flow state through anything having to do with drawing, art, painting, or puttering/organizing. She adored projects and would happily arrange them any and all times. She was, by nature, an extraordinarily constructive little girl who loved to create things. Her ability to conceive of something she wanted to do, gather the materials she needed, and break the project down into components was rare. As long as I was willing to ferry her around to get the things she needed and be a willing assistant if something was just outside of her capacities (which wasn't often the case), she was happy. When she was drawing or working on one of her projects she had this sweet efficiency about her; she was purposeful and directed, happy and humming. And she would emerge from her activities calm and centered with a sense of congruence and accomplishment. The children were able to regulate themselves through these types of play activities.

The interesting thing to me is also that their play preferences and ways of achieving these deep states were really very different. In retrospect, I realize how important it is not to put a value on how they get to this state but to understand that the ability to enter this flow state of deep play is what is really the important issue. It is also striking to me that what each of them are pursuing as adults bears a very marked resemblance to what they loved as children. Alex is at NYU getting a double master's in Drama Therapy and Counseling Psychology and Marina is at Yale getting a master's in architecture. Though I didn't know it then, Alex's room was more or less a drama therapy environment, filled with all the tools of the trade, costume pieces, symbolic props, play people, animals, and everything he needed to create his scenarios. What he loved then is what he loves now. He always turned to dramatic forms of some sort to extend his inner world, to soothe, challenge, and amuse himself, so I just followed his lead and got the things he requested. He worked out his conflicts in this way, restored a calm mood and stimulated his imagination, creating elaborate, complex games of fantasy play. And as he grew older, he learned to love to talk through what was going on in both his inner and outer worlds with those close to him. Marina, on the other hand, loved to create things. Her great joy was seeing a project through from beginning to middle to end whether it be a picture, a collage, a structure of some kind, a little book, or a cooking mission. She loved being hands on, combining elements, solving spatial or intellectual problems. What they loved then is just what they love now. Do what you love and you'll love what you do.

These states of deep play were very emotionally integrating and stabilizing. They were also more advanced forms of self-soothing and self-regulation, which are basic developmental tasks for all children to learn. Beyond sucking on something, holding a Teddy, humming, or curling up against Brandt, me, or someone else in their world, which are some of the many important ways that children soothe themselves, these deep play periods offered avenues for both Marina and Alex to self-soothe and regulate their emotional and physical states while solving ever increasing complexities of play. Because of the soothing power of trance states and the focusing, calming, and regulating effects of the flow state, these periods of deep play produced all sorts of benefits. They:

- Helped the children become purposeful and attending
- Calmed, smoothed, and regulated motor behavior
- Enhanced their ability to concentrate
- Integrated thinking, feeling, and behavior
- Modulated motivation
- Regulated anxiety and emotion: enhanced skills of self-regulation
- Engendered feelings of passion, pleasure, and ecstasy

(Amen, *Change Your Brain, Change Your Life*)

I see, with the perspective of age, how important it is to co-create an environment with our children that builds on their strengths. I was just going along with Marina and Alex's preferences to keep them happy and give them constructive activities to engage in on more or less their schedule. We came up with solutions by my letting them take the lead, in a sense, by showing me what made them happy, what kept them feeling purposeful and engaged. What helped them feel calm and regulated. And I got more of the things they seemed to like having around to make their rooms a sort of "prepared environment." I got a big kick out of watching them play happily and, like any mother, I wanted to keep them busy and content. When Grandma gave Alex his barn and animals, I became aware of how much he loved having the whole scene so that he could extend his little scenarios. I don't really think I had any idea that these might be the foundations for later career passions, but in retrospect it makes sense that what they loved as children would continue to be what lit their spirits throughout their lives. Somehow many of their developmental needs sort of got woven together through these types of activities, pleasure, passion, engagement, interaction, self-regulation, focusing, and motivation.

The Flow State

Certain passions — say, for painting, writing, sports, cooking or whatever activities we're truly engaged in — can also allow us to enter what Mihalyi Csikszentmihalyi of the University of Chicago calls the *"flow state."* In his extensive research in this area, he has found that people are most likely to enter this state when their skill level and the difficulty of the task itself are properly matched. Too little skill leads to frustration, and too little challenge leads to boredom. In the flow state, time tends to disappear, we engage in a deep, effortless involvement where ordinary cares are out of consciousness. We're receiving immediate feedback and we're goal-oriented. While in this flow state, our concern for self tends to disappear; however, when we emerge, our sense of self feels strengthened. — Tian Dayton, *the Magic of Forgiveness*

Montessori cautioned not to fill a child's world with too many adults. I witness this all the time. Marina and Alex just seemed to feel freer and happier if there weren't too many well-meaning adults clogging up the atmosphere. Though I used plenty of babysitters, au pairs, and all sorts of help over the years (and the kids got the adults to play endless games of the kids' choosing), I always valued our time just being a mom and kids. We entered a soft rhythm in the quiet of our home that we all cocreated. They sort of knew that I was only good for so much and that they would need to find ways of amusing themselves. I was a willing support for an attuned presence and an occasional (read daily but not always constant) playmate. But just being around so they could check in, just anchoring the atmosphere so that they could move around it with security and comfort, so that their world was securely tethered and would not just float away with them in it, seemed to go a long way. They didn't want only face time, though that one-to-one floor time type of connection was certainly critical and very important. But there was another kind of time they wanted to have. A just-being time. A flowing time. Time spent sharing the same atmosphere doing whatever we were doing. Home time.

The Natural Trance State

Most people don't realize that self-hypnosis is a natural state; it is an altered state that we move in and out of many times a day. Techniques like visualization can feel almost trance-like, but many people frequently go in and out of them all the time, like when we go into a trance driving along a highway or watching TV. "Self-hypnosis taps into a natural 'basal ganglia' soothing power source that most people do not even know exists," says Daniel G. Amen. "It is found within you, within your ability to focus your concentration. The basal ganglia are involved with *integrating feelings and movement, shifting* and *smoothing motor behavior, setting the body's idle speed or anxiety level, modulating motivation,* and *driving feelings of pleasure and ecstasy.*" People who have been through trauma can become deregulated in the basal ganglia region of the brain. The basal ganglia can become reset to be constantly on the alert. This is not only a phenomenon of war, but also of homes that are characterized by chaos, instability, abuse and/or neglect; all circumstances where those involved learn to be hypervigilant, constantly on the alert for potential trouble. Part of healing from these patterns is to learn to reset the basal ganglia and consciously self-soothe.   —Tian Dayton, *The Magic of Forgiveness*

Our Montessori School,
a Kid's-Eye View

When Marina turned eighteen months we started a little Montessori school in Bethany, Pennsylvania, where we were living at the time. It's still there. Beth Hubbard, who became the director after we left Pennsylvania to move to London, had a master's in art education. We gave art its own morning. One day Beth came equipped with materials for the children to make full body pictures by lying down on the paper and having someone trace around them, cutting out their body shapes, and coloring them in. Marina loved her hair. She liked brushing it, putting ribbons in it, and wearing head bands. Her Daddy bought her pretty barrettes that she made all sorts of styles out of and she admired her Aunt Anne's ways of doing her own hair and imitated them. Because her hair was so important to her, she wanted it well represented. She used almost all the yarn Beth had brought and made her hair go practically to the floor on her "self-portrait." Children have their own way of seeing things, a little wish fulfillment. Marina wanted (and probably thought she had) long, princess-like hair, and Beth let her have it through art.

When I had a parents' night at our school, I did something I would probably not have the nerve to do today. I asked the parents to spend the entire meeting on their knees and to waddle around the classroom choosing activities and seeing the world from their child's perspective. Initially they were a bit skeptical. Large men, the town lawyer and the mayor looked at me a bit askance but went along gamely for their kids' sake. They took coats off, loosened their ties and belts, and lowered gingerly down to their knees with looks of both amusement and suspicion. Who is this lady that is in charge of my children's education? The evening progressed. It took the adults a little time to warm up to the classroom (and to get around it on their knees) but eventually, just like their children, they settled in. Two thirds into the evening all parents were deeply engaged in some activity or another. I looked around the room and enjoyed the quiet hum as parents were operating happily in their children's world. The lawyer and the mayor were chuckling with pride and congratulating each other for mastering the spooning activity, getting adzuki beans from one dish to another without spilling too many, and two moms were giggling and toasting each other at the snack table, just as their little girls did each day. One dad, an accountant, was riveted by the red rods, which he was "working" with on the floor with all the concentration and pleasure of a child. That evening did more to teach these parents about the way in which their children experience the world than all the information that I might have imparted. And by the end of the evening their skepticism had completely melted away and was replaced by excitement, pride, and light-heartedness. They learned from "being there" to gaze into their children's world from their lofty heights and tune into the reality teeming through the four-foot-high orbits that their kids inhabited.

Raising Little Communicators

I didn't put Marina down for the first six months of her life. I guess I was insecure. I couldn't even seem to leave her in one room and go to another. I was so worried that she wouldn't understand that I was coming back. We could, of course, analyze me and my issues here, but I'm onto a different theme: sign language. When Marina was a baby we were living in Wayne County, Pennsylvania, God's country. We had a jeep with four-wheel drive and a tow chain, not because they were chic as yet, they weren't, but because we needed them to go to and from our home. Twice a week, a neighbor lady came over to help me around the house and with Marina. She had raised six children in the country with outdoor plumbing and a husband who drove a truck and was gone during the week. She had, in spite of it all, been an excellent mother. "They bring their love with 'em," Regina used to say. "I didn't think I could love another one as much as I loved the youngins I had, but they bring their love with 'em. They're God's little miracles."

Regina recognized a clueless, first time mom when she saw one and would try to help me as best she could. Seeing me carrying Marina everywhere I went she said, "You need to teach Marina the sign for 'I'll be right back.' 'Go like this.'" She crooked her finger, went straight up into Marina's fascinated face, smiled, signed, and said, "I'll be right back" in a seasoned, squeaky, very deliberate voice that has been living in my head ever since. Marina was riveted. Clever little girl, she learned it immediately. After Marina was six months or so old, I left her with Regina for four hours twice a week. Regina taught her "I'll be right back" and Marina learned it. An important part of Regina's "I'll be right back" was a jolly reunion: "I'm back, hi sweetheart" with lots of vocals and attention.

"I'll Be Right Back" — Using Simple Signs to Communicate

I didn't pay too much more attention to this sign language that Regina taught her, life seemed to move so fast, but I was vaguely aware that Marina didn't get twitchy anymore if I left the room and I could seem to do it, for a moment, knowing I could tell her what was going on and she understood. Years later, when Alex was born, he was sitting in his floor seat just as Marina used to do. Marina, now about three, bent over him, hinged from the waist toddler style, chubby little child arm smack in front of his face with her slightly crooked finger right in front of his eyes and said over and over again, "bye back, bye back." Then she would run somewhere, find something or do something and come back and reconnect with him with great flourish. At first I thought it was some little game. Then I realized that she was teaching him "I'll be right back." This is how she had seen and heard Regina. "Bye back" was what she had understood. Though she had not been capable, at the time, of learning the word exactly, she had completely understood the right sign, the concept that went along with it of leaving and returning and the general sound of the words. She had also recorded Regina's emotional energy, exactly. Clear, strong sweet intention and excitement upon return. As soon as she was in a situation that called for it, she reversed roles and became a little Regina, doing exactly as she had learned for Alex.

Teaching Sign Language to Babies and Toddlers

Speech therapists claim that while babies learn to speak when they are aged about one, at six months old they understand words and can make basic signs in the way deaf people do. It is thought there are about 50 signs babies can learn, but the six basic ones American speech and language therapist Diane Ryan is teaching are: more, eat, milk, pain, nappy, and help. Ms. Ryan, adds: "Research has shown babies who sign are less frustrated since they have a way of expressing their wants." Studies have proved babies who are taught a few simple signs not only speak earlier than non-signers but have larger vocabularies and become better readers.

As I reflect on it I can see my father using signs with me. He had a hand motion that meant eat. He used to repeat the motion with his hand and look quizzically at me and I understood he was asking me if I was hungry. He also had a way of asking me if I liked something, he would nod his head in a yes motion and say "kala?" with a question in his voice, "kala" meaning good. Mostly I remember that he was always curious about what I was feeling and investigating. He would move his hands in a quick circle around his own face and look at me quizzically and say "ti einai?" — "what is it" in Greek. It was the intense interest on his face coupled with the signing that I responded to. He drew me out, toward him, and I learned what he was trying to say to me. In return, I stretched my inner world toward him, becoming bigger and fuller on the inside as I did, and we would meet on a magical bridge suspended in the air between us.

I Need You Right Here, but You're in My Way

Our own research has led us to a very different insight into what has been thought to be one of life's major dilemmas: the conflict between security and dependence, and exploration and independence. The toddler's awareness of patterns and her ability to see and hear her involved, loving parents across space, supplies her with a portable emotional security blanket that permits her to confidently explore her outer world. She is able to remain wrapped in the warmth of a parent's love, even from afar. The child's growing ability to create complex patterns therefore provides a solution to this dilemma. Of course her caregivers need to be engaged and involved in these emotional signals across space to enable this process to occur in an optimal way.

—Stanley Greenspan, *Building Healthy Minds*

Both my mother and father had signs in common. Clicking their fingers meant I was supposed to stop what I was doing, as did a very particular look. My parents were lenient and easygoing so I knew to respond if my mother's eyebrow went up. I also remember their sign for come and sit next to me. They patted the couch next to them with their hand or whoever I was supposed to sit next to and I instinctively obeyed. All of these little signs helped to bring order and points of understanding into my world, and I passed them on to my own children.

"Uppie" — Becoming a Two-Way Communicator

At around five to six months, as I remember, when Alex became able to sit up he figured out how to get us to pick him up. He would reach his arms straight into the air, turn his face toward me and make a gesture and a sound. This is how he told me for months that he wanted me to pick him up. It was a wonderful, two-way communication that we shared with pleasure and purpose throughout our day together. It met a pressing need that he was communicating to me and I was responding to. And as a bonus it was accompanied by the heavenly feeling of bringing my adorable little boy into my arms. I always stole a luscious little hug as my reward and he hugged me right back. Or vice versa.

Life's aspirations come in the guise of children. — Rabindranath Tagore

---

I remember the moment exactly, when he added a word to this gesturing form of communication. We were in London, in our kitchen, having breakfast. I was busy getting food onto the table. Alex was in his high chair. When he was finished he was conscious of feeling confined and wanted to get out. I was probably a bit distracted but moved to him as quickly as I could. He made all the familiar gestures, but somehow, today, with more emotion and almost a yearning in his eyes. I was thinking (in a split second sort of way) that he must really want to get up. But what he was yearning and searching for was something else. It was a word. His first outside of Mommy, Daddy, and Mwina.

"Upppp, uppp." He said it so naturally in a way, it was hard to realize that he had just crossed such a milestone. I think he was thrilled to be able to manipulate his destiny with language.

From here, the world suddenly developed a whole new layer as he came to understand that words were a better way to get more of what he wanted than gesture alone. Alex had what Montessori describes as an explosion into language. Everything had a name, including wishes, desires, and emotions. And words were a way to communicate all of them and get, hopefully, better, fuller responses than with gesture alone.

Marina's first sentence is as clear in my mind as is Alex's first word. We were playing with her best friend, Maggie. She was around two, it was a sunny day in the country, and we were outside with Maggie's mom and the dogs. Until now, she and Maggie had been communicating through gesture and Maggie's short sentences, as she was around ten months older than Marina. Nothing had seemed missing to either of them or to her mom and me. The girls loved being together, so much so that connecting with Maggie motivated Marina's first sentence. We were all on one side of the house. Marina wandered off so I followed her.

Maggie came looking for Marina, and as she could talk she used her words as locators: "Marina, where are you?"

"I'm over here, Maggie," Marina yelled back.

As simple as that. Motivated by a perfect situation in which words were more effective than anything else in communicating. The sentence just popped out of her mouth. Marina would have probably been capable of saying that sooner had I not been so attentive (maybe a bit overly) to her every need or had I thought of playing hide and seek or something. But no matter, her first sentence was clear and precise and fully formed. Another milestone. I was amazed. Marina has always had the ability to project her thinking toward other people and situations. Hearing Maggie calling for her and knowing she wanted to find her let Marina complete the pattern of communication across space. There is nothing that is more motivating to children than doing what they want to do. Alex really wanted to get "up" and Marina really wanted to be with Maggie.

Letting kids lead the way into activities that interest them helps just about everything. Small and large muscle coordination, interactive skills, gesturing, language development, emotional development, motivation, and two-way communication. All of this is brain growth in one way or another.

Many forms of development happen more easily when children are doing what they want to do because it means they are purposeful and motivated. And a purposeful motivated child is an attending child.

Alex was a born communicator and very interested in connecting with the people around him. This trait showed up immediately. Brandt used to walk the children around in the evening to calm them. This was something that, by the end of the day, I just couldn't do. Dads are great for this more active type of thing. Anyway, Alex from before he could hold his head up would just fix his little face on the back of Brandt's neck until Brandt turned around and talked to him. Then Alex's face would burst into a smile that covered his whole head as he tried to hold it steady to keep his Dad in view.

The same thing happened when I breast-fed him. He wasn't nearly as interested in food as he was in eye contact and heart-to-heart connection. He loved to know he was connecting with us.

Meta-Messages and Body Language

When Marina was upset with something she would pull her bottom lip up and tilt her little head. Alex's feelings were generally written all over his face, and if I didn't notice them he would make some fed-up physical gesture like stomping his foot and pulling his arms down. The children told me with their eyes and body when they wanted something long before words entered the picture. First gesture and body language, then words double coded with emotional meaning and intention.

We communicated by gesture, smile, grimace, hand signals, body language, touching, body positioning, reaching, pushing away, lifting up, putting down; all the myriad of physical interactions that combined together to make an integrated web of communication. And each of these "gestures" had an emotional meaning double coded into it. As they grew, this meta-language became more and more complex and its meaning more and more intricate. We still communicate this way, all people do. I can see at a glance how my kids are feeling, and they have only to look at my face to know what mood I'm in, how I feel about what was just said or done, and if I'm with them in the moment or somewhere else. All this without a word.

Even the deer in our field teach signs. At first light the mothers and fawns are eating in the hay field. At some mysterious moment, the mothers give a sign to their fawns and little spotted heads with ears sticking out of them sink straight down into the hay field. You wouldn't be able to see them unless you walked right over them. Hours later when the mothers return they deliver some sort of sign from at least fifty feet away, and the second they do, two little ears with eyes attached pop straight up, out of the tall grass.

Raising Kids Who Can Separate and Stay Connected

The most important thing parents can teach their children is how to get along without them. — Frank Clark

One of the important developmental tasks kids need to learn is how to separate and stay connected, how to be able to be with their parents and eventually others and on their own while still keeping that feeling of connection alive inside of them. Healthy communication helps us to do just this. We learn to communicate across space in ever increasing increments, to stretch that bond so that it can sustain us while still allowing us our autonomy. I have very clear memories of Alex moving toward and away from me from the age of one to the age of two. We had just moved to London during this very important phase of development. Alex was securely attached to me, I would say. He knew I was his for lack of a better way to put it and I knew he was mine. We belonged to each other, hands down. We had an "us" space that felt hearty and loving and warm. During the first half of that second year I could almost see Alex's ability to recognize patterns develop. He could understand the layout of the house and go from room to room. He remembered the routine of our morning and held me strictly to it; especially going to the park at nine-thirty after Marina went to school. He was able to hold the experience of me inside of him and move away from me with confidence.

Gesture: Our First Form of Communication

Gesturing is the interactional language upon which all later communication is built. Before language even enters the picture, we have learned a rich tapestry of gestures to communicate our needs and desires. Each of these gestures is double coded with emotion and is stored by the brain and body with emotional purpose and meaning attached to it. "Adults who have not engaged in adequate gestural communication as toddlers frequently have trouble with certain abstract concepts. Many adults in therapy have a difficult time identifying some of their intentions and emotions. . . . During the course of therapy we discover that some patients have more interactive experience with certain emotions than with others. They may recall warm exchanges with their parents when they were young, but remember very few discussions around aggression and assertiveness. Their families may have thought that such feelings were dangerous or frightening and avoided expressing them with their children or with each other."

— See Stanley Greenspan, *Building Healthy Minds*

This grew by stages. In London at the park he would venture from my side as soon as we reached his familiar playground, in search of toys, friends, and adventure. He began by getting to the top of the slide and then signaling me wildly that he was there. Next was the top of the jungle gym. He would climb to the highest rung then yell to me to see. He could happily be apart for growing periods of time, carrying the experience of care and security inside of him, checking back when he needed to, to make sure his anchor was still in place. Alex would get to the park and shoot out as soon as his feet hit the ground. After eight or ten minutes he sort of realized that he'd been on his own for a while and he'd come to me for what Margaret Mahler called "refueling." He refueled by leaning against my crossed legs, resting his arm on them and keeping a watch over the goings on of the playground. Then his emotional tank would suddenly be full and he was off again. Eventually he was happy to go to the park with a babysitter and a friend if the time away was not overly long.

Productive Shame vs. Nonproductive Shame

As our children get on their feet, and start to get into anything and everything, they hear the word "no" from us around every nine minutes. "Observational studies show that 12-month-olds receive more positive responses from mothers, while 18-month-olds receive more instructions and directions," says Schore. It used to be that psychologists suggested limiting access to situations that might lead to these shame messages. But these exchanges can actually stimulate complex brain growth. Researchers today recognize that these can be productive learning sessions if the parent helps the child to recover quickly from the negative impact of a shame message and find constructive ways out of it, e.g., we yell "no" at our child about drawing on the wall, they feel shame, then we get two sponges and clean it off together.

It's important to understand "the growth-facilitating importance of small doses of shame in the socialization process of the infant," says Schore. "Embarrassment (a component of shame) first emerges around 14 months, when mom's 'no' results in the child lowering his head and looking down in obvious sadness. The child goes from feeling excited about what they're doing to deflated by the sharp 'no' they receive." During this rapid process, various parts of the brain get quite a workout and experience heightened connectivity, which strengthens these systems. The result is development of the orbitofrontal cortex (cognitive area) and limbic system (emotional area). These two systems can then interrelate to build emotional resiliency and the ability to self-regulate emotions and impulse control.

What is important to remember about productive shame reactions is that there must be a quick recovery. Extended periods of shame result in a child learning to shut down, or worse, become hyperirritable, perhaps even violent. If the shame messages go on without relief or repair our children just learn to go numb. But if the attuned mother feels a pang of sadness seeing her little one's obvious deflation and attempts to use this as a teaching, reparative moment, then these become little lessons in self-regulation, resilience, and perhaps even growth in values and morality.

"Neurobiological studies indicate that these constant 'no' messages are shame inducing and that episodes of shame like when we yell 'NO' at our children and they hang their heads, can actually stimulate the development of the right hemisphere, the brain's source of creativity, emotion and sensitivity, as long as the shame period is short and followed by a recovery. In essence, it's not the experience of shame that can be damaging, but the inability of the parent to help the child recover from that shame."

— See Joanna Lipari, Psy.D., "Existential Treatment for Chronic Depression"

Throughout Alex's forays into the world was my ever-present tracking of his movements. Because he was a kid who plunged into the activities surrounding him, my task became to watch his participation as he made the many small adjustments that the situation inspired and required. If he was doing fine, I let him find his own way. If he went too far or put himself in a risky situation, I would let him know that in whatever manner the situation called for, then I'd work with him to find a better alternative and together we would try for some sort of new approach or behavior. Something that fit the circumstance. Gradually he learned how to regulate himself on his own so that he could fit himself comfortably into situations apart from us. He could happily go off with other families, babysitters, and later preschool and integrate himself into those worlds.

I have memories of Alex checking in and waving from the top of so many places: the top of a small cliff with other boys in Connecticut, the top of a skinny little tree outside a movie theater in Minneapolis, the top of a very tall pine in upstate New York. Alex could separate and carry us with him, which allowed him a lot of freedom. He learned how to find us when he needed to check in by refueling, waving, and eventually by phone.

Raising Kids with Emotional Rudders

> *Nobody, not even the rain, has such small hands.*
> —e.e. cummings

In one of our many conversations about what we want this book to do, Roy Carlisle, whose idea this book was, said something that I thought I'd just paraphrase here. He was talking about how smart, brilliant, caring parents often miss something very crucial about teaching their kids self-regulation and emotional literacy, especially as life moves so fast these days. "Many parents don't understand that teaching a child self-regulation is what we do from the very beginning," said Roy. "They can't see that teaching an infant who can't even talk how to self-regulate actually means teaching them how to be an adult who can self-regulate.... They also often don't see that mothers (and fathers) need to regulate *themselves* if they want to have kids who can do the same . . . they need to understand that . . . just paying attention to a child is so powerful . . . it means so much to tune into them, follow them into their world and try to understand what might be going on."

It's hard to realize that these little thirty-pound beings are really in the midst of arguably the most powerful learning curve of their lifetime. But they are. The learning they do during these first years will last them a lifetime. The caressing and cooing that we think they won't even remember will, in fact, become part of their innermost being.

A Walk in the Park

Spring has come to New York and Central Park looks like it's in the middle of a baby boom. Proud parents of each and every type are pushing their babies, legs and arms flailing and falling out of strollers — the ones who've become too big over the winter for their little mobile nests — dropping things from extended hands that their parents scurry around to pick up. The little babies all look like this might be the first outing of their lives, snuggled under white blankets with soft hats tied under their chins, little squished-up faces barely peeking out at the world. Then there are the toddlers lost in wonder at anything from a dog passing by to an especially riveting crack in the sidewalk...or staring, staring, staring apparently dumbfounded, deep in the utter rapture of the moment as they witness another little person, maybe a foot or so taller than they are, throw a ball. "What skill!" I imagine they're thinking, "how did they ever learn it?"

A little further along ...oh, oh...a little girl sitting astraddle on her mother's lap, face to face. "I don't have the words so I will show you, Mommy. Watch carefully as I demonstrate how I'm feeling, I'm curling my lip now and tucking in my chin, I'm making little whiney sounds and staring down waiting for you to read me and help me to decode this stuff inside of me. Pick up my signals, Mommy, see me on the inside, read me accurately and help me to feel held as I sit here full of feeling on this lap that is the most important place in my world. Know me, sense me. Love me even when I am like this, petulant, needy, insecure...just hold me and let me know everything will be all right because I believe everything you say, oh Mommy of mine, who holds the keys to the entire universe." And as this scene continues to unfold, I see that the mother is, in fact, guarding

her little girl's personhood with her own body, intuitively mirroring the child's facial expressions and creating enough space
on her lap for her daughter to wiggle and pout her way back
into the normal day. Teaching her to regulate her inner world
until she finds her own emotional rudder so she can balance
and steer through her inner currents. Sitting with her as she
learns to tolerate the strength of her feelings, holding her until
she learns to hold herself. And then, as if some inaudible bell
has rung that no one else can hear, it's all over. She slips off
her mother's lap like a seal sliding off a rock and returns to her
play, returns to life.

Next we pass a little grouping wandering along in the general direction of the zoo. Mother, father, and grandparents chat
as a little girl appears to be bobbing up and down behind them
like a buoy in a harbor. As if they are all on some sort of invisible
raft and she is splashing about in the air behind her mother's
languid arm, anchoring a floating family. The clan continues to
proceed down the road, seemingly unaware that one of them
is dragging along in another flight path all together. At first
glance I want the family to slow down and enter, en masse, the
cosmos of the little space cadet in their midst. But as I watch, I
realize that that arm, that lifeline, is part of what is making her
little orbit so safe and wondrous. That acts as a sort of surge
protector, connecting the two worlds so that she can safely release herself into her own mysterious and magical universe,
content in knowing that her connection with the world she will
gradually live more and more of her life in is kept secure.

The Opiates of Love and Attachment — How Nature Supports Nurture

Intimacy with our children makes us feel good all over for
some very physiological reasons. The atmosphere of closeness actually affects our body chemistry producing seratonin
in both mother and child. Seratonin is the body chemical associated with states of calm and an overall sense of well-being.
Touching produces oxytocin, the "touch chemical" associated

with feelings of calm and serenity. Nature rewards attachment with soothing body chemicals or endorphins that reinforce the parent/child bond. The experience of having a child has been referred to as having your own heart running around the world on two legs. Erica Jong referred to her "little balls of DNA 'whirling through space.'" All I can say is that motherhood, for me, was a corporal experience. My whole body felt different. I felt settled as if, well, as if motherhood were somehow sort of soothing. Life seemed softer and more centered. Things that used to bother me fell away because my children seemed so much more central to everything that felt important. My life had a core, warm and glowing, that vibrated with vitality and immediacy. Nothing was what it had been, everything had moved into a different place. My children were the foreground and the rest of the world slipped into the background. I more or less judged everything I did in terms of how it did or didn't fit into the family life that was now becoming so central to my identity.

Bonding with other women who had children was some "enchanted moment" seeing someone across a crowded room and "flying to their side." How old is your child? Does she sleep through the night? How long since you've had any sleep? How much longer do you think you can stand it? How is your sex life? Do you still care about it? OOOH did you see what she just did, isn't that the cutest thing you've ever seen? So full of hope and promise, so alive. All with the unspoken undertone, "Are you experiencing what I'm experiencing? Did your world just undergo a seismic shift, did you feel the earth move under your feet, too? Did the trap door to your soul suddenly spring open like mine did?"

Being in this close and comforting world with my children felt like the answer to a prayer. It grounded and connected me both with the most ordinary of life experiences and with a sense of destiny or eternity. It ensured my place in the scheme of things and taught me what it meant to love. It drew me out of the small me toward the larger me and rubbed off my rough edges like an agate in a tumbler, till I became smooth and lustrous.

In my children's eyes I was someone and so I stretched and struggled until I could fill the shoes that they set out for me. They made me humble because I worried constantly and about everything. I felt incessantly out of control, persistently worried that something could happen to these little beings who meant more to me than anything ever had. Motherhood, the great leveler. All mothers wear their hearts on their sleeves.

We all experience a release of the body chemical oxytocin when we touch each other. (Men experience it, too, but testosterone undermines it.) This is why, as women, we gather together with each other and our children. And as we gather and touch and then gather and touch some more, even more oxytocin gets released, rewarding this experience of connection and making us want to keep it going. Think of little boys, too, before testosterone takes over, they play like puppies jumping around and rolling all over each other. All children do. The oxytocin that gets released acts as a fertilizer to the brain and body promoting all sorts of neuronal growth. Nature takes care to reinforce those experiences that are good for us and punish those that aren't.

I heard a World War II veteran say that he'd had countless soldiers die in his arms. They all called out for their mothers with their last breaths, he said, each one. That's why it's so important to be as good a mother as you are capable of being, because we are imprinted on the souls of our children, wired into their neurobiology, stamped on their hearts.

Self-Soothing —
Learning to Manage Your Inner States

Learning to self-soothe is a primary developmental task for all of us. When we can't self-soothe in healthy ways we look toward unhealthy ways to attain that "feel-good" state. Working for the past three decades in the field of addictions has provided me with endless examples of how people who don't have a well-learned ability to soothe themselves attempt to solve that problem. Drugs, alcohol, food, sex, and spending are quick and easy. They calm a jagged mood or medicate a hurting heart but only for a while, till they wear off. Then the mood is still there and the hurt has gotten bigger and sprouted legs.

The Critical Importance of Touch

There is a singularly comforting body chemistry to being hugged by a parent who loves you. If a mother monkey scoops a baby close against her chest, heart rates drop. When scientists measure stress hormones, they can chart them dropping away. An identical reaction can be seen in human children. A child tucked against his mother's shoulder seems lulled into that easy chemistry of contentment. One of the scientists who has done the first and best work on the chemistry of touch is Saul Schanberg of the Department of Pharmacology at Duke University. Schanberg suggested that our intense response to touch is a primitive survival mechanism. "Because mammals depend on maternal care for survival in their early weeks or months," says Schanberg, "the prolonged absence of a mother's touch triggers a slowing of the infant's metabolism." That allows the infant to survive a longer separation from the mother. Once she returns, her touch reverses the process. Premature babies who are stroked for fifteen minutes, three times a day, grow 50 percent faster than standard, isolated preemies. The baby who huddles into his crib, or the little monkey who curls up at the edge of her cage, appears hopeless. But we should be aware that some of this huddling is actually conservation. As they hunker down, the babies are waiting for their mothers to come home and for everything to be all right. The bottom line is that touch is good for your health, your immune system, your sleep, your anxiety level, your life."

—Deborah Blum, *Love at Goon Park*

How Our Body Processes Emotions

The limbic system is associated with our emotions and the neo-cortex is associated with critical thinking. Both are operative in processing emotions. While the neocortex can collect facts quickly, the limbic brain does not. Physical mechanisms are what produce our experience of the world and we need new sets of physical impressions to change or alter those impressions. When we have problems in our deep limbic system they can manifest in mood-iness, irritability, clinical depression, increased negative thinking, negative perceptions of events, decreased motivation, floods of negative emotion, appetite and sleep problems, decreased or increased sexual responsiveness or social isolation.

— See Daniel G. Amen, *Change Your Brain, Change Your Life*

Children learn how to regulate their inner states from being around what psychologists call "an adept external regulator." Namely us. We teach this skill to our children by how we manage ourselves and how we manage them. Internalizing the ability to self-soothe is something all children need to learn and all adults need to practice. Children have a variety of ways, as any mom knows, of soothing themselves. They may hum to themselves, suck their thumbs, curl up with a blanket, read, listen to music, play, or engage in doing something they enjoy; rest with a movie or play quietly doing one of their favorite activities. These activities allow them to calm themselves and regulate their own internal states. Even receiving or witness-ing acts of kindness, exercising, relaxing, or doing meditation releases seratonin in the body. This is why our children need calm environments to grow up in with plenty of kindness surrounding them and reasonable regulated schedules. And why we need to remain reasonably calm ourselves, so that they can learn self-regulation through the way in which we handle them from moment to moment. Because the opposite occurs, too.

Stress chemicals that make us boil up inside can be created by homes where yelling, constant criticism, rushing, chaos, or neglect takes over. Creating a calm environment for our children to grow up in can be one of those silver linings of motherhood. As we establish a soothing atmosphere for our children to internalize, we become calm and regulated, we feel good, too. We both learn and practice the skill.

Raising Relaxed Kids
The importance of downtime

Of all modern notions, the worst is this: that domesticity is dull. Inside the home, they say, is dead, decorum and routine; outside is adventure and variety. But the truth is that the home is the only place of liberty, the only spot on earth where a man can alter arrangements suddenly, make an experiment or indulge in a whim. The home is not the only tame place in a world of adventure; it is the one wild place in a world of set rules and tasks.

—G. K. Chesterton

Alex was in third grade. Most of his friends were signed up for after-school activities but he wasn't interested. When I asked him why, he got this very ancient, faraway sort of look in his eyes as he stared out the window. "To be honest, Mom, I don't have time."

Me: "You don't have time?"

Alex: "Not really. I have a lot to do."

Me: "A lot to do?"

Alex: "Yeah, I need to play with my friends in the building, watch some cartoons, have a snack and relax. I need to play in my room by myself, see you for a while. I don't have time. Besides, all day people are telling me what to do, where to sit, when to talk or not talk, I have enough at school, I like to come home and just do what I feel."

With that his eyes came back to normal, he swiveled around and returned to being an eight-year-old boy hard at play. I was stunned. He had so clearly articulated his life as an eight-year-old. And he was right. He did need to do all those things and there just weren't enough hours in the day, he had to make some choices and the ones he made seemed reasonable to me. Children tell us what they need if we listen. Alex later loved after-school sports, but on his own developmental schedule. Not third grade but by fourth he wanted them.

Both Alex and Marina are good at keeping themselves occupied, happy, and self-motivated, I think because they learned to do this as children.

The Accident

When Alex was five he got hit by a car. I was at the Museum of Natural History's cinemax with Marina and friends waiting for the babysitter to bring Alex to join us when I got pulled out of the film by a phone call. It was someone from some drugstore or wherever the call was coming from saying, "Your son has been in a car accident. Call this number. I don't have any more information." Finding a phone from which I could call out on were among the longest few minutes of my life. I called what turned out to be a policeman and he immediately said, "He's fine, a couple of broken bones that's all, he's talking to me, he's a great kid. I'll pick you up at the corner of 81st and Central Park West immediately and take you to the hospital." Marina stayed with Monica and her mother at the film. I could barely find my way out of the building, it seemed like the walls were moving. I cried all the way to the hospital. The police woman told me not to let Alex see me crying. I assured her I felt just the same way and that's why I intended to cry all the way to the hospital so that I could be strong for him when I got there. And there he was. My brave little Alex lying in an emergency

room. His beautiful little five-year-old self, courageously holding together, strong and articulate. "I wish you had been there,
Mommy." "Me too, Alex, I wish I had been there. I am here now,
what can I do for you?" Alex tucked me into him and we just
stayed there physically close and connected through the next
scary hours while they poked him, hurt him, x-rayed him, and
so on and so on. My friend Alexandra had seen the accident
and gone with him to the hospital and she called our friend
John Cornwall, M.D. Both came to the hospital as did Brandt
as soon as she got a hold of him. Thank God they were there.
Eventually we went up to the ward of the hospital that he'd been
taken to as it was the closest to the scene of the accident. It
was scary and Alex was in pain. Everything was a fight. A de-
cent room, kind treatment. TV we had to pay for and wait till
whenever they got around to supplying it the next day. It was a
long night through which Alex was the pluckiest, most upbeat
little patient you could ask for.

The next day Alex made a discovery that, as fate would have
it, laid a foundation for things to come. In the playroom were
two drama therapy interns. As soon as Alex connected with
them I felt a great sigh of relief. They gave me my first true
moment of rest and lifted some anxiety through their kindness,
caring, and effectiveness at working with him. They made an
attempt to connect with his heart and mind, not just do things
to his body. Through play they allowed him to tell the story of
what happened to him. He had very limited mobility because
his leg was broken in three places and still uncasted, but we
wheeled his whole bed into the play room and he participated
as fully as if he had been able to do everything. He loved the
fantasy play and showed the therapists what had occurred by
using dolls and toys. They let him relieve his fear by showing
his story, and by playing in any way he wished to. He could
release and relieve his anger, aggression, and sadness through
play. With their gentle, heartfelt guidance, he used dolls to play
out a safely distanced scene of the crime. He fought back and
regained a sense of empowerment by fleeing for safety and
acting on his urge to run, in play, at least, if not reality. He took

to this immediately and it turned his sense of victimhood and fear around. Eventually our TV was turned on and it seemed that every kid on the ward arrived at our room for seven a.m. cartoons. Alex made friends, asked for play dates (they climbed into his bed with him or wheeled up to it) and maintained a cheerful mood in spite of his pain and immobility.

Our next challenge was going home and still having six weeks ahead of us in a full leg cast, then another six weeks in a half leg cast. More painful procedures. More immobility. It was hard for Alex to face the summer he had so been looking forward to without being able to do the things he was excited to do. Alex went through those first six weeks with crutches and a wheelchair, which he stopped using the first week. There was a lot he couldn't do. It was frustrating and difficult to greet the summer with a hot cast and be deprived of doing all his favorite things. It was traumatic to have gone through an accident. He was scared to cross any paved area at first but got over that. At first we got him a gerbil so that he could have a little animal that didn't run too far. But the most successful thing we did was to start him fishing. In his full leg cast, Alex would stand on the dock of a nearby lake and cast for hours. It wasn't at all unusual for him to cast for six or eight hours with breaks for lunch. He would go into these meditative states, mesmerized by the lake and the casting and the fishing. He caught our dinner over and over that summer. And fishing has never left him.

When it was time for his half cast he was incredibly relieved. It was called a walking cast but in his case it was a running cast. He ran races against other kids and won, did back and front flips off the diving board, and jumped on the trampoline. The doctor had told me his leg was safe and he could do his normal things. Well, these were his normal things.

At the same time I tried to continue some role-play whenever the accident came up. He bashed up a few plastic vans to get his anger out. But the most healing moment came after his cast had off been off for many months. I was giving him a bath and he began talking about his accident, he didn't often mention it so I made use of the moment. "If that water spigot were the van, what would you like to do to it, Alex?" He nearly pulled it out of the wall. I quickly dried him off, grabbed a pillow, put it on the floor and said, "this pillow will represent the van. You can do anything to the pillow that you'd like to do to the van." I also told him that he could use bad words (which he loved to experiment with but was not allowed to use; I wanted to pull out all the stops and have him feel fully gratified). He hit, stomped on, threw, cursed, out and generally yelled at the pillow for a very long time. I "doubled" behind him. Doubling is a psychodramatic term we use in role-playing. It consists of standing behind the "protagonist" and giving voice to the part of their inner world that they may not be expressing, bringing it into conscious awareness, so to speak, and then letting them take over. I doubled things like, "You hurt me, you knocked me down and scared me, you were careless and it hurt me." Alex took over and spoke out all of his hurt, anguish, fear, and anger. "I'm just a little boy, you should have been more careful. I had to have all that pain, it was scary, you did a bad thing" and so on. Gradually he came to a position of feeling less helpless and at fault, more empowered. Marina, in the next room, came in to see what was happening.

"Marina, this is the van and I'm getting mad at it."

"Can I have a turn?"

"Yeah, yeah." Alex grinned and cheered as Marina expressed her own feelings.

"You bad van, you hurt my brother and he had to miss doing all his fun things and you're bad and I don't like you," and so on.

"Thanks, Marina," said Alex, feeling protected and vindicated. I asked for a turn, too. "You hurt my son and I am furious with you. You caused him all sorts of pain, he had to be so brave and you weren't looking. You really did a bad thing," and so on.

As all of this progressed, Alex became more and more free of the pain and anger he was carrying inside and felt increasingly supported and understood.

"Can I give the van to the dogs, Mom?"

"Sure, Ali," I said, hoping that the dogs would somehow figure out what to do. Alex came running in from the kitchen, thrilled, saying, "They're protectin' me, they're protectin' me." Unable to imagine what he meant I asked what they were doing.

"They're lyin' on it so it can't move." Alex led me out to the kitchen, where Otter and Minky, our two black and tan miniature dachshunds, were passed out on the pillow snoozing deeply, which still, in Alex's mind, clearly represented the van. He was overflowing with feelings of being cared about, vindication, relief, and renewal. As we returned with cups of cocoa to watch a favorite show and cuddle in, I doubled for Alex again.

"I feel powerful."

Alex spun his head toward me. "I feel powerful," he said.

"I feel strong," I doubled.

"I feel very strong," he echoed. "And I feel better, I'm not scared any more, I feel good in my feelins." Alex often referred to his "feelins." Alex had done drama therapy and psychodrama at home and accrued all of the benefits, a shift in perception around himself and how he now viewed what had happened to him. A catharsis of painful emotion, integration of new insight and meaning, and a restored sense of spontaneity. Emotional repair. Re-empowerment. The next day Alex came to me and said, "I feel sorry for that man who hit me, he must feel so bad, maybe we can tell him I'm okay." His healing was deep.

Raising Little Choice-Makers

> *It is essential for students to recognize that they have choice about their thoughts, feelings and actions. Generally it is the hardest thing for them to accept that they have this choice. Only from this understanding, though, can they learn real accountability.* — Karen McCown

One of the things my mother used to say to us all the time was "learn to make your own decisions." I recall not having a clue as to how to do that when she said it, but I liked it. It felt grown up and clever and respectful. And, as children do, I worked out my own child-sized method using my feelings and ideas as guides or pointers that helped me to figure out what I wanted to do next.

Marina and Alex each had their own way of becoming choice-makers. I could almost see their wheels in motion as they felt their way toward whatever they wanted to eat, do, or have. I could see them mentally and emotionally trying something on for size and then a light bulb would go off and they would just know. Or know they didn't know yet and might need to give it some time or space till they did. Allowing and training the ability to make choices is a big part of good parenting. We want our children to grow up being good choice-makers. Choosing what to wear, what to buy when at the supermarket, and what to cook for dinner teaches them how to become choice-makers. I involved Marina in every facet of choice-making possible. And when Alex was born, we would literally discuss all aspects of what to do for him. Was it time to change him, did he need a blanket, was he hungry? Anything to involve Marina in the process so that she didn't feel marginalized any more than necessary. Each time of the day that a choice might have been appropriate we made one. With each of them, I generally boiled the choices down to three or so and let them decide which sandwich, outfit, plaything, piece of fruit, treat, and so on they preferred. This helped them both to feel autonomous and to learn to see options in their world and act on them.

Child-Friendly Decorating — Setting Up a Manageable Environment

Marina's Room

My Montessori training greatly influenced how I set up Marina's room. Everything in it was child-size and everything in it could be operated by her. Her drawers were at her height. She had little cupboards to keep her things in and shelves for books, toys, games, and playthings.

I studied everything that went into their little worlds. I looked for clothes that Marina could put on herself, as much as possible. Big buttons that she could manage and develop hand dexterity, easy to use zippers or pullovers that pulled on without making her contort into a pretzel while I tugged her body all over the place. I looked for slip-on shoes or Velcro until she could learn to tie. I got clothes with big pockets for her little hands so that she could carry around her treasures.

And we set her room up in the same ways. All of the furniture in Marina's room was child-size and she was able to operate it. Unpainted furniture stores proved to be a great source of this kind of furniture. I bought small bureaus, cupboards, shelves, and a child's table and chairs and painted or stained and oiled them. Some I covered with Rit dye in pretty colors, then put a coat of wax or polyurethane on top. I also put a strip of wooden pegs at a safe and accessible level so that she could hang her nightgown and bathrobe on it. Her bed was always close enough to the floor so that she wouldn't hurt herself if she fell out of it. Marina took great joy in keeping her room, as she called it, "nice and neat." A Virgo, Marina naturally loved order and systems and had her own way of doing things from the beginning, often superior to mine, I found. And generally superior in her mind.

We picked out the colors, wallpaper, and rug together. It was her room and she took pride in it. I used to narrow choices down to a few I thought would work and then let her choose the one she liked best.

We created a corner in the kitchen that was hers, also. This corner was especially important because it was downstairs and close to the action of the day. It gave her a place of her own to go to that was in the middle of things, not banished. We had a small set of three shelves, a beautiful wooden child's table, and two chairs that I'd found at some sort of antique/second-hand store, and refinished. On the shelves we had baskets and trays. The baskets were low and small and the trays were child-size. In each basket and on each tray we had separate activities. Whenever Marina felt like she wanted to do some particular activity, she would look over her shelves and peruse what was on them. Once she decided what to do she would remove a tray or a basket from the shelf, put it on the table, and "work" with it. Montessori felt that children wanted to feel a part of the world and taken seriously, so she referred to children's activity as their "work."

I still remember clearly, as does Marina, what was in some of those baskets. One of her favorites had a small rolling pin, a large ball of play dough, cookie cutters, and a plastic knife. Another basket held colored markers and paper, another a matching game, another dominoes, one had a doll and some clothes, one origami papers with paste and child scissors for collage-making. It went on like this. And when I cooked dinner I often gave Marina a little something to "work" with that she could manage. She had a little cutting board and a plastic knife to cut bananas with or something else she could manage, and there was always some part of dinner she could contribute to. Marina and I passed so many hours of pleasure and companionship like this.

Alex's Room

The way we set up Alex's world was different from Marina's. He had different likes. Alex, from the get-go, loved characters. When we'd go to the Museum of Natural History he would study the stone tools made by early man, then spend the entire weekend searching for pointed rocks, whittling sticks, and finding pieces of leather to bind them together. He'd spend the weekend dressed in a coonskin cap making and using his tools. When we watched a Superman movie, he would disappear and come flying back into the room in his Superman pajamas. If he was watching Daniel Boone he sat there dressed in his Daniel Boone outfit, surrounded himself with all his tools, and asked me to heat up a can of beans, which he ate out of a tin pie plate.

Needless to say, Marina's room would give Alex no pleasure. The only similarity was the size of the furniture, not that he ever put his things away in it. For Alex we built a small loft that he could climb on. He had a tent in one part of it, kept his tools in another, and had lots of other things I rarely saw because I didn't climb up there much. We had several pegged boards on which we kept his variety of hats (cowboy hat, coonskin cap, army hat, fox fur hat, headdress, crown, ninja cloth, super-hero head gear, and so on). On another pegged board we hung his various costumes, Karate Kid, Daniel Boone, Superman, Spider-Man, etc. Still a third pegged board held his holsters, magic belts, bow and arrow, GI Joe belt, red sash, etc. We also needed a tray for his sheriff's badge, camouflage sticks, ninja star, Native beaded necklaces, homemade tools, sticks, stones, you name it. In the footwear department we had GI Joe boots, beaded moccasins, and cowboy boots (at least). The other end of Alex's room was all fantasy play. He adored and collected toy soldiers, super-heroes, every kind of animal. He had barnyards and mountain ranges and toy trains and castles. He reveled in endless and elaborate games in which he played all the roles. I would have loved to watch him more but when I opened the door he ordered me out before I could enter. His world was filled with a soft light, and an electric sort of energy that made it seem as if fairies were flying all over his room. It gave off a glow.

Raising Kids Who Can Relate

> *It is a great mistake, I think, to put children off with falsehoods and nonsense, when their growing powers of observation and discrimination excite in them a desire to know about things.* —Annie Sullivan

Marina had her own little plastic, yellow, pink and blue, shopping cart that we took with us to the grocery store. I was a little self-conscious as this was before the phenomenon of child-friendly carts at stores across America, but it kept her so happy and involved and it was light and easy to throw in the car.

(In fact it lived in the car.) She followed me around (or I followed her around) as she picked out the things she thought she or we might like to have from the grocery shelves that were at her level. She learned to read first the big letters on the front of packages and eventually the labels on the back. She discovered how to shop for groceries, check for healthy ingredients, and generally take care of herself. And we had fun letting her choose. (Shopping together is still one of our favorite activities.)

Treat Family Like Friends and Friends Like Family

It is a common experience for people to get along and function well in their network of relationships in the world and poorly in their families. They are unhooked, less invested, more objective and expect less from their network of friends and workers. If people would examine how well they function in some areas of their lives and make the translation to their close family relationships, they would improve their function in the family 100 percent. Expectations may get the job done but the emotional climate is stifling. Decades from now we will all be dead. What will it matter if the beds were made or unmade. What will matter and influence people long after we are gone is the emotional legacy we leave to our children and through them, to their children. This will have influence when we are all forgotten. It is these unworkable levels of expectation, largely transmitted through the generations, that turn people off.   — Thomas Fogerty

When Alex was two we moved to Greenwich, Connecticut, for a period. Having just come from London, we didn't have too many friends and he didn't want to go near a nursery school. The parks that cities have and all the kids play in didn't really exist in the suburbs. So we spent a fair amount of time just the two of us when Marina was off at Whitby, her kindergarten. Alex, as do many two-year-olds, took great pleasure being useful and helpful. One of the ways he did this was to empty out the cart when we were at the grocery store. He would sit inside the cart and put things, one by one, onto the conveyer belt. Now this is just one of those activities that can be seen in two ways, as helpful, which was what he was trying to be, or as completely in the way of adult speed. But to ask Alex to sit on these wonderful instincts and suppress his urge to participate in a meaningful way in the real world would have been to miss a big developmental moment, in my opinion. First, he took joy in being helpful and doing something that mattered in the adult world. His face lit up each time the cash register clanged. Next, we learned lots of words from naming everything that came out of the cart. He learned how commerce took place, how to connect and interact with the cashier, and how to select and buy groceries. And he became curious and interested in his and our world so that when we got home he wanted to help me carry the groceries into the house, put them away, and begin to prepare the food we had thought about and selected together.

You can't buy a lesson in self-esteem or math like this one. You just have to see them and make use of them as they come along and to break the world down into manageable parts. Let children hold what they can hold, carry what they can carry, and do what they can do.

I took to shopping off hours and in Cos Cob, where the grocery store was owned by Italians who understood that these were the riches of life. I waited till there was no one around and they were happy to let us be slow; they enjoyed the whole event right along with us and generously played their part, too. The lessons Alex learned about translating the connection he had with me to useful activity, how to take care of himself and manage in the world, were wonderful. And we had fun. Lots of it.

Years later, when he was around eight, Brandt took Marina, Alex, and one friend each to the country while I was out of town. When I checked in with him to see how he was managing, he told me that they had just come back from grocery shopping.

I had floods of images of keeping track of all of them, along with pangs of guilt (and relief) that I hadn't been there. When I asked him how he managed he said, "the girls were easy, they had lists of everything they wanted and just went around getting them and I gave the boys walkie-talkies and sent them on missions to find things." The image of two boys in camouflage clothes "reporting in" from the cereal isle and conducting reconnaissance around fruit and vegetables was just too delightful. Dads have their own wonderful way of solving things. The kids had a great time grocery shopping, they made a dinner they loved, and the world continued spinning on its axis without me spinning it.

The Family Dinner Table
Our children's first social world

Home is not where you live
but where they understand you.
— Christian Morgenstern

A family who prays together, stays together.

When Marina and Alex were small we ate dinner together almost every night. Brandt was an art dealer at the time and had lots of evening commitments but would come home, have dinner, and then go out again. When I went back to work I tried to work only one evening per week. On weekends we planned lots of our social time as a family, having dinner with family friends, going to movies, having play dates and sleepovers (constantly), and generally having fun together. I was keenly aware that we had a very short window when our children actually wanted to spend time with us and that if we missed that window, well, we would miss it. And in due course, our children found us boring, tedious, hopelessly outdated, and not the people on whom they wished to lavish their serious hang-out time; in short, they became typical adolescents. But before that, in those honey-soaked, golden, stressful, exhausting, magical years, when we were their favorite people in the world, I lapped up the opportunity to be together like a cat with a dish of milk. I knew it was precious and I knew it wouldn't last. We had adventures.

Eating Together

* Bonds family members

* Socializes children — This is where children learn the art of conversation and manners, not just table manners but how to listen, how to talk, how to take turns in talking and listening, and how to behave in a group.

* Creates a forum where values can be communicated

* Is an automatic check-in for the day — This is where parents can hear about the children's day, track how their week is going, and tune in on their kids' lives.

* Passes on family values and rituals — For example, you may pray before meals, teaching children to make worship and celebration a natural part of their day. This adds another dimension of bonding as the family now shares something that is larger than themselves. If you are a political family, politics and current events can be discussed. If you are a literary family, conversation can turn to books, plays, and films. Most families are a combination of many of these. The subjects discussed at the table teach children how to conduct themselves in polite society.

"Marina...remember in London we were filling in afternoons together, looking for things to do that felt fun and cozy? *Star Wars* and *The Empire Strikes Back* were both at the corner movie theater for all winter it seemed. We saw both of them every week. One box of minstrels for each movie. Sitting in the front rows absorbed in adventure. Caramel and chocolate bursting into our mouths, laughing at our favorite parts and getting scared about the princess, then seeing her prevail. Passing an afternoon together just in pleasant friendship and easy companionship. Or when you were very small and all of our days were planned around your rhythms and our activities were all made Marina-sized. That sweet excitement you took to anything you wished to do? Cupcakes, magic bars, and brownies? Because those quiet, seemingly simple little moments are what sustain me now, they are mine forever as well as yours. They are what built our sense of trust and fun and relationship so that when the forces of hormones and peer pressure and growing up started to pull us apart, we were joined in our root systems. We had something solidly and consciously built that could not be easily destroyed. And Alex, picking you up at noon and figuring out what to do with you as a ball of energy was both overwhelming and heavenly. The Museum of Natural History was our constant fall back if we didn't have a play date for you or with another mom and child. But those times grabbing a hamburger together. Watching you stare at the menu, read the words and pictures, and taste every offering in your mind, being so excited over a hamburger, fries, and Coke, making small talk with you that wasn't small at all, that is what I hold so close to my heart today. That is my relationship with you, which is mine to keep. All those times that seemed so ordinary were so not ordinary. They stand out in my mind's eye as some of the best moments of my life. Just to be together enjoying the simple pleasures of life, watching you discover the world and learn to navigate it, take joy in choosing just what you wanted to eat, walking around to all your favorite exhibits, feeling proud, exhausted, inadequate, and more important and alive than I'd ever felt in my life."

Alex's palate went from being very kid-like to being very sophisticated. He became a true gourmet by eight or so, always searching the menu for foods he hadn't tried, snails, sauces and taste combinations he could explore. This enjoyment of food followed him through his years. As a young boy he was an experimenter with tastes. As he got older, he began to cook delicious things for himself. He was just good with food, a sandwich or omelet he made just tasted better than someone else's.

Chemicals Released by Playing Fertilize the Brain and Body

Play is defined by researchers as an activity that encourages positive emotions and allows people to complete high-order relational goals, such as getting to know each other, learning about each other or engaging in a mutual interest together, at a higher rate than expected. Play is accompanied by smiling and laughter, and should also allow participants to control their onset and their offset in the activity. In other words, play is not forced; it encourages autonomy, spontaneity and creativity. Friends or couples who play together report feeling greater intimacy and closeness. And this sense of closeness develops at a faster rate than normal. Adults spend too little time at play according to research, and would benefit greatly from spending more time at it. In the workplace, for example, "adult play helps to alleviate boredom, release tensions, prevent aggression, and create workgroup solidarity," says Norman C. H. Wong of the University of Hawaii. It also facilitates organizational learning, creativity, community-building and group cohesion, and overall, enhances adaptiveness, attentiveness to quality and performance. — Tian Dayton, *The Magic of Forgiveness*

As our kids got older and less excited to be with us we took them out to restaurants as a bribe and often included their friends. Both Marina and Alex are lovely, easy company. They hold their own, tell a good story, take and yield the floor gracefully, listen empathically, and laugh out loud. They are great companions and learned much of how to be that from the time we spent together as a family and with relatives and friends. Being Greek I had been raised to include the children. Greek people are very child-centered and family-focused. I didn't leave the children at home if I could take them with me because I had learned from my parents and relatives that children learn the world at their parent's knee and that the best way to teach them manners is to bring them into social situations and let them learn by doing and modeling. Including children in anything and everything seems to breed a kind of comfort and naturalness in being part of the world. A self-confidence that they have a place. Like learning to ride a bike, the fretful and frustrating early beginnings fade away and what is left is what feels like an ability that just comes naturally. Early learning weaves itself into the very fabric of our being and becomes a part of us forever. Our children went out with us, traveled with us, and accompanied us to restaurants and parties whenever possible. They are both lovely socially, handle themselves beautifully, and have lots of friends.

Raising Kids Who Can Enjoy Life

Whenever we are doing for the child, what the child can easily do for himself, we are in the way of his development.
— Maria Montessori

The sun was streaming in on our party of babbling, eating families at a Labor Day picnic at Alice's. The adults were chatting on blankets while the kids ran circles around everything, food in hand, exploring the world we were sitting in from angles we'd long ago lost sight of. They were leaping around, climbing, running, hopping, and generally zooming in and out of the scene, arm in arm, hand in hand...yelling, laughing, quarreling...and just, well, having a picnic. Our pleasant reverie was broken by an ear-piercing shriek. Had there been any glass hanging from the sky or trees, it surely would have shattered. Everything went still and all I remember after that was foot-sledding down the side of an embankment with another parent, Michael, faster than either of us had ever moved before. Within a minute we were at the children's side, responding to what we thought was an alarm signal, only to discover that someone had seen a snake or something. All was well. Phew. Relax. Adrenaline normalize. When I looked up at the steep hill I had just descended, I decided to stay below for a few minutes, just to see what they were up to and to regain my now completely lost composure.

We were a motley group of explorers ranging from eight to fourteen (and late thirties), gamboling along a sun drenched stream, hopping on rocks, getting our feet soaked, drinking the cool liquid surrounding us, picking up sticks and shiny stones. Slipping, laughing, shouting, and tripping over the rocks and water and sand. I entered into a state of mind with these kids that I had forgotten was part of the world I daily inhabited. One that lay within our reach but beyond it, somehow. Colors were brighter, the sun was magical, and all the world seemed to conspire to create one perfect, liquid moment that felt endless, timeless, and filled with aliveness. I watched as Alex, Marina, and their friends became one with something extraordinary, moving in and out of the moment as gracefully as if it were being spun around them just for their pleasure. I'd forgotten that there was such music in the universe. Such beauty at our fingertips. This sun-soaked perfection warmed not only my skin but my whole spirit as the child in me woke up and joined forces with the children I was with. Oh, Alex and Marina, is this the world you enter when you play? This limitless, alive, and creative reality, where everything flows from moment to moment in what feels like some prearranged, exquisitely orchestrated stretch of time that has emerged from a parallel universe? Is this play?

I was aghast when I realized that this altered state of reality was what my children meant when they talked about wanting to play. It was a rare and gorgeous experience that has stayed with me all these years. A perfection. A flow state. A moment of deep integration and bonding. I felt so close to all the people we were with, their faces looked so beautiful, and we were all sharing an experience that felt mood- and mind-altering, but none of us had imbibed anything besides sunshine and brook water.

Learning the Skills of Relating through Play

"If we as parents want to support the full range of our child's emotional experience, we must consider all broad areas of emotional functioning, including dependency, pleasure, love and intimacy, curiosity, assertiveness and exploration, protest and anger, and self discipline (and eventually, self punishment) as well as emotions related to these broad areas such as (the various types of feelings of) loss, sadness, anxiety, fear, shame and guilt," according to Stanley Greenspan, M.D., in *First Feelings.* This range of feelings characterizes not only children's functioning but much of adult functioning as well. When we work with our children, understanding their full range of emotions, we can begin to create a foundation for emotional literacy that will serve them as adults. It is all too easy to go for the obvious, to take pleasure and pride in the child who is producing good grades and is captain of the team, and ignore her fears of failure and dependency. Understanding the full range of affect allows us, as mothers, to help our child to build strength not only in the obvious, but what goes on behind the scenes as well.

Play is that enchanting, magical, liquid space where children and animals learn countless skills critical to their survival. They make a thousand choices in the space of a few moments as they glide in and out of altered states. They learn how to pick up other people's subtle signals and to read and react to them. They learn how to communicate their needs, wants, and wishes and to read the signals of others. They learn how to operate in a constantly shifting relational moment and to continuously and spontaneously adapt themselves to it. Both children and animals play from early infancy. All mammal brains work with a punishment and reward system. Play lets young children and animals learn critical survival skills and so mother nature has seen to it that this activity, in particular, is highly rewarded. Play strengthens connections between neurons in the brain that can actually make someone a more intelligent, fit, and successful adult. There is a powerful relationship between play and opiates in our brain or brain fertilizers. Without these molecules the brain cannot connect up properly. We know that some of these molecules are turned on by touch. Play and intimate mothering involves constant touching, says Jaak Panksepp, neuroscientist of Bowling Green State University.

Raising Kids Who Can Deal
Making discipline a chance for learning

*Emotions are a critical source of information
for learning.*
—Joseph LeDoux

Gramma gave Alex a child tool kit when he was around five. It had a few basic tools in a cute wooden box with his name on it. I didn't think too much about it at the time. He did. One day I was sitting in his room with him and I glanced over to his chair. It sat there looking sort of postmodern, a curved back with no rungs. Lovely, really. Elegant even. As I looked at it, though, it struck me as odd that someone would design a chair that you would fall out the back of. Then it dawned on me. This little boy, who still had trouble tying a knot on his shoes, might have latent carpentry skills that were well beyond his years.

Mom: "Alex, did something happen to your chair?"

Alex: (*Guiltily*) "Doesn't it look nice?"

Mom: "Didn't it used to have rungs in the back, here?"

Alex: "But I didn't like them."

Mom: "Did Carmen know you were doing this?"

Alex: "Yes, she watched."

Tian: (*Leaving the room*) "Carmen, Carmen?"

Carmen: "Yes?"

Tian: "Do you know anything about how Alex's chair came to have no back on it?"

Carmen: "Yes" (*Smiling now, in a very strange way*) "he didn't like it the way it was."

Tian: "He what?"

Carmen: (*Very slowly and deliberately as English was still difficult*) "He was esawing . . . esawing . . . , and I said (*waving her finger to show me*) 'No, no Aleeex, you must not esaw your foorniture.' (*Again smiling*) Then he said, 'I can't help it, I hate my foorniture.' (*Looking triumphant, from explaining it so well and shrugging her shoulders with a resigned smile*) What could I do?"

Tian: (*Incredulous, suppressing a mixture of horror at the thought that she allowed this and pride that my five-year-old could saw so well . . . and was, after all, showing some distinct leadership skills*). "What could you do? Well, you could have said 'no' and taken away his saw; it's only seven inches long." (*But this line of conversation was getting me nowhere. Clearly I needed a new babysitter.*)

Anyway, I had a long discussion with my boy prodigy. He explained his simple, straightforward reasoning to me. He really had never liked his chair and now he had a saw. I suggested that though we could get a new chair this once, if he sawed all of his furniture he might not have any to sit on. This somehow made sense to him. I did tell him that although he had done something he wasn't supposed to do and should not do again, I couldn't help noticing that he had done a beautiful job. He told me all about how he had accomplished this amazing feat. I couldn't help being proud.

A couple of weeks later we were sitting around the dining room table. Alex disappeared into his room and came back with his little saw. I watched him as he came over to one of our lovely, English walnut dining room chairs and poised his saw very carefully just at the very edge of a rung, turned his adorable, winsome, expectant face up in my direction with a quizzical little look that only meant one thing. "Don't even think about it," I said. Quickly he withdrew his instrument of destruction, smiled sheepishly, and said "I just wanted to see."

Lesson learned.

Alex and Anger: The Party

We were having a party. It was a lovely evening, the setting glistened, the food was prepared and the tables and chairs were set out around the garden. All was peaceful and organized. I had a fun babysitter to play with the kids and they each had a friend so that they would be happy. Ideal. Guests arrived at good intervals and soon there was a real buzz, the party was going beautifully.

As evening fell we lit torches and began to bring out the dinner plates. Then a sound broke the pleasant lull of chatting voices. A loud sound. A horn honking constantly, to be exact. In the middle of the country it sounded increasingly out of place. At first I tried to ignore it and keep up my hostessing duties. But it didn't go away. It kept getting louder. The lovely crescendo of the party started to get a bit frazzled around the edges as heads turned to and fro trying to make out the source of the din. Even the champagne was not sufficient to put a gloss over this growing dissonance. Finally, I followed the noise to the other side of the house and there was Alex. He had hoisted himself into the van (nightmare) and was sitting in the driver's seat with an expression of sheer anger and determination. He was lying on the horn with his entire upper body, yelling into the cacophony of sound. "I'm angry, I'm very, very angry. I'm really mad."

"Alex, what do you think you're doing?"

"I'm expressin' my anger."

"You're driving everybody nuts, is what you're doing. Get down from there, immediately." At this point, Alex (who was very strong, you'll remember) was hanging onto the steering wheel with both hands. I dragged him, arms and legs flailing, and stood him on the ground. "Alex, what are you doing?"

"You told me to find different ways of expressin' my anger."

"Not these ways, other ways."

"I was just doing what you told me to do."

"I didn't mean honking the horn. I meant learning to talk about it when you're angry."

"I am talking about it while I'm honkin' the horn."

"Okay, we'll talk more about it tomorrow. Why are you so mad?"

"Kathryn and Marina won't let Keith and me play with the cabbage patch dolls."

"Okay, I'll talk to them, and you can, too. Tell them you're angry and feel left out."

"Marina, I'm angry and I feel left out."

At that point, everything took a turn for the better. The next day we talked about ways of expressing anger that were a little less, well, disruptive. Alex admitted that it felt really good to express his anger but he understood he'd need to do it without the horn, next time. He would have to find other ways of feeling powerful when he was feeling marginalized. He could ask me for help if talking didn't work.

The good thing about this was that Alex got to know what the edge of his own anger felt like and it gave him a sort of confidence to talk about it in more ordinary ways. Knowing he could really get it out, so to speak, seemed to make it easier for him to find a middle ground. He had heard the sound of his own loud voice and felt what he was capable of so he could make some in-between choices.

Actually, Alex became quite good at saying he was angry and setting boundaries without going too far. I am always amazed at how engaged his thinking is; even when he is in the heat of anger he remains reasonable and clear headed.

Tell Me No Lies

Marina went through a period around seven when she loved to jump rope. It was her twirling, jumping phase. She never entered or exited a room without a twirl or two and she carried her jump rope everywhere, just in case. (It was around this time that she also wore a bathing suit to school under her uniform every day. When I asked her why she wore one as her school had no pool, she simply said that you never know when a pool might appear and she wanted to feel prepared.)

Anyway, she wanted to jump rope in the foyer with her au pair. She thoughtfully asked me if she could tie one end of the jump rope to the credenza and Ruthie could twirl the other end while she jumped. I said "yes" without too much thought. After a couple of days of jumping, they broke our expensive, antique chandelier. The rope had caught on it. Her au pair was expecting me to yell at Marina (and maybe her). I later learned that her au pair was really upset with me for not getting mad, but how could I possibly get mad at her for breaking a glass globe I hadn't even thought to consider? She already felt very bad for breaking something lovely that she liked as we did. Something pretty in her home. And she was as responsible a girl as anyone could be. Why would I make her feel even worse than she already felt? And why would I want to teach her to fear me and avoid telling me how she felt? If there was fault it was on all sides, and breaking a lovely object was sufficient punishment for a caring and careful girl like Marina who took better care of her things than I did. She needed reassurance, not yelling. Her "super ego" or that part of her that was a rule-setter and discipline-maintainer was already strong enough. She needed nice, understanding voices to incorporate to offset how hard she already could be on herself when she made a mistake, not harsh ones. She had disciplined inner voices, plenty of them, and she needed soft ones to make her own and "no big deal, it's okay" voices.

Alex needed something different, help in understanding the consequences to his actions and strategies on how to respect things and act and express himself constructively.

But my goal with both Marina and Alex was first to keep channels of communication open, and to do that I had to keep the big picture in mind.

I was napping, or rather trying to rest a bit one tired afternoon. Alex and Keith came creeping into my room looking sheepish.

Alex: "Mom, I have something bad to tell you" (*seeing a look of panic come over my face*), "not too bad, just kinda bad."

Tian: (*Feeling relieved now, realizing that something had been demolished, nothing more*) "Yes?"

Alex: "Well, Keith and I were playing catch and by an accident the ball sort of fell out of my hand like this (*He mimed the ball falling out of his hand*) and by an accident it fell kinda fast and by an accident it bumped into the window and by an accident it went through the window."

Tian: "Are you trying to tell me you broke the window?"

Alex: "Just one of the little windows that you hardly see. And just a little hole, not a big one. (*Oh, that's a relief.*) It was all an accident, Mom."

By this time Alex was looking so adorable and trying so hard to impress upon me that it was "an accident" (you may have noticed) that it was not difficult to maintain my composure.

Tian: "Well, Alex, I'm sorry that we will have to repair the window, that will cost some money and be a hassle and I would like you to be more careful next time when you play ball and play away from the windows. But thank you for telling me the truth, that's what's important."

Alex and Keith looked very relieved. The two of them threw their arms around each other's shoulders and walked out of the room. As they did I overheard Alex telling Keith, "I told you she wouldn't get mad." I couldn't believe my ears. I had actually succeeded in withholding anger at small transgressions enough so that Alex knew I wouldn't get mad.

A wise man had told me when Alex and Marina were young to tell them that I would only be mad at them if they didn't tell me the truth. *They could come to me with anything they had done and I would not get angry as long as they told me the truth.* This set the habit up for them to tell me if something "bad had happened" rather than hide it. When they were young that meant broken dishes, stains on furniture, and broken windows. But as they got older it became much more important. When Marina's friend got drunk in eighth grade and started to vomit uncontrollably the girls called us mothers and a doctor. When Alex's friend was sexually intruded upon and didn't dare to tell her parents Alex told me she needed help. When their friends were experimenting with alcohol and drugs they knew they could tell us if they felt they were getting in above their heads. I have always felt grateful for that very fine advice. It taught my kids to tell the truth and kept the door open for them to reach out for help before things got out of hand.

Raising Snowflakes
Being a different parent for each child

There is no creature whose being is so strong that it is not greatly determined by what lies outside of it.
— George Eliot

Parenting isn't one size fits all. Each child requires his or her own unique set of strategies.

I remember when Marina was in second or third grade. Teachers love kids like Marina who are mature and responsible, who play ball. She was an excellent student who loved school. She loved her desk, her pencils and erasers, she was crazy about folders and notebooks. She liked my three-ring hole punch and knew how to use it by the time she was seven. She made teachers like teaching and she made me feel like a competent mother. On the inside, Marina was always stretching to understand the demands of any circumstance so that she could meet them. This was an enormous strength that she is still able to bring to any situation. But it can be wearing to be so good and competent. I saw one of my tasks with Marina to get her to be okay with not being okay. When teachers disciplined her (which was almost never) she took it very seriously. I told her getting kicked out of class wasn't all that big a deal. She said she didn't want to stand in the corner. I told her standing in a corner didn't have to be so bad, you could count spider webs, have a little break.

Being bad once in a while didn't have to mean she was bad.

I remember when she was in fourth grade. She used to come home every single day and complain about one girl in particular who would say mean things to her. For weeks I felt indignant along with her, coddled her, tried to understand, explain and commiserate. Eventually I got sort of tired of hearing all of this and began to wonder if I was creating a funny mentality by us connecting so much around this issue. I decided to try something different. The next time Marina came home and talked about, we'll call her Lisa, I said, "I'm happy to talk about Lisa, but from now on, I don't only want to hear only about what she said to you, I want to hear about what you said back."

The next day, literally, we spent two minutes on what Lisa had said and twenty on what Marina said back. The day after that, two and ten. Then one and five. Then, on to another subject. It wasn't actually helping Marina for me to be only a "good listener and comrade," I decided, she was somehow getting disempowered by it. She needed to have permission to act out a little, too. To meet this girl head on. It changed not only the dynamic between them but the whole constellation of kids. Lisa had been quietly bullying and all of the kids were sick of it and rallied around as soon as Marina took some sort of stand. It, I feel, strengthened her. Life, after all, isn't always easy. Sometimes you have to be a little tough.

You Get What You Expect

Scientific studies reveal that positive expectations yielded positive results and negative expectations yielded negative results. This, in parenting, is a bit of research that goes a long way. Expecting good things from our children can become a self-fulfilling prophecy, as can expecting negative things. Part of a mother's spiritual discipline is to learn to see the good in her child and to draw that out; to learn to identify a child's special gifts and help the child to bring them forward and actualize them. God has placed gifts in each and every one of us. Seeing these gifts in our children and helping them to come forward is part of the work of spiritual mothering.   — Pierce Howard, *The Owner's Manual for the Brain*

Alex was different from Marina. Let's just say, I didn't need to encourage him to be naughty, he found his way there all on his own. Alex, being a half-Greek male, had a natural disdain for being told how to spend his time. He had a lot of his own ideas on how to spend it and school wasn't necessarily one of them. I always thought I started him too soon in nursery school, at three. I wouldn't have, actually, but we'd just moved to Manhattan and it seemed the thing to do. Alex was as social as the day was long so that part of school worked well. I highly valued the fact that Alex was the kind of kid who, at home, was never bored. He had lists of things in his little mind that he wanted to do and would order them in his head. On weekends, in the country, all he needed was a friend and the woods and he was endlessly happy. It really bothered me when Alex would get disciplined because I felt terrible sending a kid like this to school where he had to conform to a schedule and eventually sit in a desk. It seemed so unlike him. I found him schools that suited him and that helped a lot. And he was such a sweetheart that friends and teachers liked him.

My tack with Alex was different from my tack with Marina. It was to try to get him to tow the line as comfortably as possible, to help him get on board with rules and schedules and to figure out strategies to make them more tolerable for him. I wasn't great at this, actually, but luckily things worked out anyway. Basically, the more independence he had, the happier he was, which meant, by the time he hit college, he knew himself and understood how to organize his life to stay on top of things. He knew to have his own dorm room, for example, in sophomore year and to put off having a car. Just to remove temptation. He got around just fine without one. Then, when he got a house as a junior, he got a car and he took care to live in an atmosphere that allowed him to keep up with his studies.

Talking things over at length all through Marina's and Alex's childhood helped them to learn from the circumstances in their young lives and apply what they learned as they matured into adulthood.

Marina and Alex needed to decode their days, especially when they were small and really wanted to talk with us. When they got to be teenagers, words were like pieces of gold, and they gave them over sparingly. So these young years when they're waiting to come home and decode their days with Mom or Dad are very important in terms of building relational skills and emotional literacy. You build literacy using the situations in your child's day as the instruction booklet. Generally I tried to listen a lot. We'd bat things around together, discuss options. I tried to keep advice (I rarely succeeded, probably) to a minimum and see if the kids could come up with their own way of handling a situation, using skills from their own tool bag. Working with Marina and Alex insured that the lesson would be right for their level of development because we were breaking down concepts and applying them to situations as they came up in their own lives. It also, over time, taught them how to reflect on both themselves and their life circumstances, learn from them and use them as fodder for personal growth.

Just as children learn more words from being talked to as youngsters, they learn the concepts of emotional literacy through talking things through in the course of their developmental stages. Nothing is more important to teenagers, for example, than themselves. They are ripe for learning about their inner worlds, for going within and decoding the twists and turns of their minds and hearts.

This approach also teaches the spiritual idea that our lessons are always right there in front of us, sewn into the lining of our personal experiences. We just need to learn to see through the right lens, to tease out the meanings that are laced into the situations of our own lives.

Getting Your Act Together

If you bungle raising your children, nothing else you do in life much matters. — Jacqueline Kennedy Onassis

During my training as a psychologist, I ran into a term that I have carried and treasured for twenty-five years: "The Good Enough Mother." A British psychoanalyst called D. W. Winnecott coined it to describe the mother who was neither preoccupied with being supermom, nor neglectful of her duties. She was not necessarily up on all the latest parenting techniques, didn't create an unusually enriched environment, didn't try to raise astrophysicists or corporate giants. She was just a mom raising her kids as best she could. She was good enough. Good enough to give her child what was needed to get him or her from one stage of development to the next, good enough to provide enough basic security so that the child could form trusting bonds. Good enough not to ruin her kid, which, let's face it, is the modern mother's worst nightmare. I found this phrase so comforting. I remember hearing it with a sort of awe. You mean I don't have to be perfect, that my child will make it through life even if I flub up once in a while? My personality or lack of awareness or tons of other things I don't think of won't necessarily cause irreparable damage to this child whom I love more than life itself? You mean good enough is good enough?

Nature is with us on this one. Our children are programmed to meet their emotional developmental markers in much the same way that they're programmed to crawl, walk, and talk. We don't need to invent anything, just to support and work with what nature already has going. Emotions were coded into us to help us survive. Fear to keep us from running headlong into the proverbial saber-toothed tiger and a desire for human connection to insure the survival of the species, which we experience as love.

Emotions are the elusive elixir that gives everything in life its taste and flavor. They guide us toward one person or experience rather than another, tell us what we like, what we wish to avoid, and what brings meaning and passion into our lives. They are as necessary to our living as food because they insure our survival.

Being a Pleasable Parent

Marina and Alex brought a kind of joie de vivre into my life. I had always had a capacity for enjoying life and experiencing emotional depth, but becoming a mother blew my circuits. Nothing till now compared with it. My capacity for joy (as well as work) simply expanded. My heart enlarged. My soul grew. My children brightened up my day, my month, and my year. My experience of what it meant to be *in* life changed.

I can think of countless ways that Marina used to take pleasure in pleasing me. A picture that she rushed to show me, making me sweet presents, getting my positive response for anything from saying a word for the first time to mastering a task or leaning into me for comfort and contact. She was so highly motivated by the attachment bonds she felt with Brandt and me to learn, grow, be productive, clever, and accomplished. Though accomplishment came naturally to her, she was also a typical first child and took pride and pleasure in delighting us. And we were delighted; boy, were we delighted.

I felt deeply thrilled each and every time our children showed signs of meeting their developmental markers whether it was sitting upright, moving objects from hand to hand, or taking that first step. I recall Alex standing against the coffee table. We were sitting around chatting with Grandpa and some cousins when suddenly, he walked from Grandpa to us, striking out for his first steps with the determination of an explorer crossing an arctic sheath. I remember him grabbing my face with two hands and turning it toward him so that he could pull me from my distractions, get me to listen, and study my expression. Or when he did something clever or cute, his little upturned features quietly fixed in my direction to see if I was impressed. I have so many memories like this I wouldn't know where to start or finish.

———⟐———

> If the child is to keep alive his inborn
> sense of wonder without any such
> gift from the fairies, he needs the
> companionship of at least one adult
> who can share it, rediscovering with
> him the joy, excitement and mystery of
> the world we live in.   —Rachel Carson

———⟐———

And they span time. This wanting to please their parents has motivated our children from day one. This one lasts a long time. Well into adulthood I wanted and needed my mother's, father's, or grandmother's admiration and it felt great when they gave it to me. This one is also gender free, which really says a lot about the equal importance of the mother and father in the inner life of the child. Our appreciation is very motivating for our children, they need to feel that they can please us and we need to be pleasable parents.

Over the years as a psychologist, I have come to recognize how important it is to children's developing sense of self

and self-esteem to feel that they bring pleasure and happiness to their parents. It becomes a template that lives inside
their heads. Then, even when we are not there they are driven
to do those things that they know we would love them to do.
If we don't corrupt this natural urge on the part of our children by expecting the impossible or being constantly critical
or controlling so they need to spend their life in quiet (or un-
quiet) rebellion, this can be a motivating force that our kids
internalize. It can become a sort of self-fulfilling prophecy. At
some level they feel they please us and unconsciously they expect that the rest of the world will also find them good little
people. Children who feel they disappoint their mothers or fathers never quite get over it. They spend their lives searching
other people's faces for signs of displeasure until they eventually create it. But bringing that glowing, satisfied smile to
the mother's, father's, or grandparent's face gives a child a
kind of inner confidence that can last a lifetime. They feel empowered by it. Strengthened. Important. And the opposite, a
disapproving, critical face, can also last a lifetime.

   I remember picking Alex up from school when he was small
and seeing his turned up face looking into mine. What he met
with was invariably my genuine pleasure at laying eyes on him,
reconnecting after hours of separation. I recall both of them
almost bed height, first thing in the morning, tapping on my
sleeping arm, "It's morlin time, you can wake up, you want" —
waiting for me to open my eyes and smile, at which point their
faces would start to glow. "Here I am, Mommy, your gift, your
special person who has the secret key to your heart. Look at me
and feel good inside." To grow up the apple of your mother's
or father's eye is to carry a confidence into adulthood that lives
at and emanates from the center of your being.

   Once when Marina was saying good night she turned to me
and said, "What's bigger than a heart? Is there anything bigger
than a heart?" "Well, a soul, I guess, is bigger than a heart,"
I replied. "Then good-night, Mommy, I love you with all my
heart and soul." How had Marina gotten it at such a young
age? This expanded and ever growing capacity for love that

happens between a parent and child. How did she know to think it through and name it? "Good-night, sweetheart, and thank you for naming this overpowering, bigger than anything feeling. I love you with all my heart and soul, too."

Actions Speak Louder Than Words

Children have never been very good at listening to their elders, but they have never failed to imitate them.

—James Baldwin

Children watch their parents like hawks. They hunt for inconsistencies. If we say one thing and do another, or profess to hold certain values and demonstrate other kinds of values, they pick it up and they either get confused, hate us for it, or become like us or twist themselves into understanding little pretzels or enmesh themselves into us so that they don't have to suffer the pain of experiencing our inconsistencies. Or some of everything.

Part of becoming disillusioned in your parents is a normal, healthy growing-up process. Our kids are forced to see us as real people, warts and all, and to integrate their normal and natural conflicting feelings of love and hate toward their parents. They see us as flawed people whom they love anyway and eventually, this helps them to love and accept themselves and others.

However, if we are too inconsistent, if we give them images of us that are too far opposing to integrate, or deny the reality they are experiencing or our own bad behavior, they feel crazy inside. They become caught in a loyalty struggle between their natural drive to love and look to us and their innate intuition that what we are doing is off or wrong.

Remember, children come to us straight from God. Their moral compasses have been set from above and they are ready to trust on sight. And they do. So we must be trustworthy enough to demonstrate being the kind of people that we want them to become. We teach far more by what we do than by what we say. The right words need to be grounded in the right actions in order to impart clear and meaningful lessons. Children need to experience love to know the meaning of the word "love." They need to be able to depend on a responsible parent so they can internalize the meaning of responsibility and learn to be responsible themselves. We need to walk our walk not just talk our talk if we want our children to grow along the right lines. Even when we do everything as well as possible, our children, today, still have a world that all too often demonstrates violence and immorality. Without a firm grounding from us, their chances of following on a good path are even more compromised.

When I am tempted to do things that I know aren't right I ask myself this question, "What will it feel like to look into my children's faces knowing that they know what I have done?" This is a good question to ask myself. It straightens me up rather quickly.

Spiritual living calls on us to demonstrate. It is not enough to say I love you; we need to demonstrate our love on a daily basis. It's not enough to say be a good person; we have to show our children what that means by being one ourselves. It is not enough to say the right thing. We have to do the right thing or our words make a mockery of the lesson we are trying to impart. We need to show them the difference between right and wrong by how we act and by owning wrong behavior in ourselves and apologizing for it. In this way we teach them that it is okay to be human, to make mistakes if we can own them and make reparation. This is why we have a forgiving God, because life is full of this kind of rupture and repair, falling down and getting up, wounding and healing. Loss and redemption. Describing closeness in words is meaningless, we need to show our kids what a healthy, intimate relationship is by how we behave in our relationship with them and with their other parent. None of this has anything to do with perfection; it has to do with reality. Our children live and grow in the reality of the way we live, not in abstract concepts or conversations. Who we are and what we do is what communicates our values to them most clearly and effectively.

Parenting Is 90 Percent Show and 10 Percent Tell

I always say that parenting is 90 percent show and 10 percent tell. The danger in talking about emotional literacy as merely a language is that we might learn to say all the right things but not do them. Our words have no weight if we don't back them up with meaningful actions. Demonstration of love is what puts the point across, and that demonstration is constantly taking different forms.

I remember when Alex was hit by a car and we were rushed to a hospital, there was a baby in the room opposite him. Hung on this baby's crib were several balloons saying "I love you" and new little dresses and sweaters. In the week that Alex was in the hospital we never saw one relative visit that baby. Those balloons became a mocking symbol of what should have been there but wasn't. Someone knew they were supposed to have or express these feelings but the baby's world was empty. She wasn't talked to or held or connected with. She lay there, helpless, words of love floating in the air above her crib but no one showing her what love felt like. No arms to enfold her, no cooing voices, no touch, smell, or feeling of a person loving her; nothing that demonstrated the experience of love so that she could learn through her senses what love is really all about.

Love assumes many forms, as any mom knows. Sometimes it's showing up on time to pick our kids up from school, greeting them with open heart, missing them, cooking their favorite foods, cooking them what is healthy for them, tucking them in, maintaining order, taking them to the doctor or dentist, disciplining them, comforting them, listening, talking, laughing, touching. Love takes so many forms. But the important thing is demonstration.

Talking to Your Children
Grows Emotional and Cognitive Intelligence

◆ A child is born with over 100 billion neurons or brain cells. That's enough neurons to last a lifetime, since no more neurons will develop after birth. These neurons form connections, called synapses, which make up the wiring of the brain. At age eight months an infant may have 1,000 trillion synapses. However, by age ten years the number of synapses decreases to about 500 trillion. The final number of synapses is largely determined by a child's early experiences, which can increase or decrease the number of synapses by as much as 25 percent.

◆ The brain operates on a "use it or lose it" principle: only those connections and pathways that are frequently activated are retained. Other connections that are not consistently used will be pruned or discarded so the active connections can become stronger.

◆ When an infant is three months old, his brain can distinguish several hundred different spoken sounds. Over the next several months, his brain will organize itself more efficiently so that it only recognizes those sounds that are part of the language he regularly hears. During early childhood, the brain retains the ability to relearn sounds it has discarded, so young children typically learn new languages easily and without an accent.

◆ The power of early adult-child interactions is remarkable. Researchers found that when mothers frequently spoke to their infants, their children learned almost 300 more words by age two than did their peers whose mothers rarely spoke to them. However, mere exposure to language through television or adult conversation provided little benefit. Infants need to interact directly with others. Children need to hear people talk to them about what they are seeing and experiencing, in order for their brains to fully develop language skills.

- Researchers who examine the life histories of children who have succeeded despite many challenges have consistently found that these children have had at least one stable, supportive relationship with an adult early in life. This is based on the research on resilience by Emmy Werner.

Babysitters, Au Pairs, and Other Needed Helpers

When we lived in London, we'd go to the park every morning. As soon as we got there, Alex would strip off most of what he was wearing (the English are far more relaxed about this sort of thing than we are in America; children on the playground are expected to look like little ragamuffins, then they clean up marvelously for tea). Absolutely everything about Alex's park time was sensorial. The sand beneath his toes, the dirt he dug in, the bars he was constantly climbing, the slide he scooged or sailed down and the dirt he landed in. He dug holes, built sand piles, and generally made a splendid mess that helped him (and me, I suppose) to feel alive and aware of his world. In-between, he'd come to tell me something, show me something, but mostly to lean into me from where he could regain his bearings and plot his next move. Alex used me as a sort of high-backed couch, leaning against my crossed legs and resting a folded arm against them as he perused the scene to decide which play circle he was going to wheedle his way into. Once he had figured it out, he'd make his move. He had a whole little system worked out in which he would sidle up to a little group and stare at whatever it was they were playing with. After they got used to him standing there he might just sit down and slowly begin to enter whatever activity was going on or maybe he'd get a subtle invitation to join from one of the kids. Seamlessly he became a part of groups in this manner and the next scene is always of Alex playing happily as one of them, as if he had been there all the time. This ability to become part of things kept morphing into new and more adult shapes as Alex grew.

Marina loved the one o'clock club — a little corner of Holland Park where at one o'clock, moms and nannies gathered with their little ones and two or so park teachers brought out paints and activities that the kids could do if they felt inclined. Marina loved paint, clay, or anything with gluing, cutting, pasting, and pipe cleaners. She would be absorbed for ages, chatting with her friends, meeting who was beside her, watching, showing, fixing, shaping, busy-busy-busy. She found anything artistic to be visually and sensorially exciting. She loved all things art-like. She had a real sense of aesthetics and knew just how she wanted something to feel and look. She was social through these activities in the same sort of way Alex was social through larger body motion. They just came alive when they were engaged in activities that involved all of their senses.

———=◈=———

> Never show a child what he cannot see.
> While you are thinking about what will
> be useful to him when he is older, talk
> to him of what he can use now.
>
> — Jean-Jacques Rousseau

———=◈=———

I tried to be there to let them "touch base," as my mother calls it, and move out into the world again. I only worked with babysitters and helpers who seemed to understand how to be supportive and responsive. Often that meant they weren't as helpful in other areas but I felt less guilty if I left the children with babysitters whom they saw as large playmates than if I left them with, well, "cloth nannies," people who were physically present but psychically absent. It was a little harder for me as I picked up more of the practical slack, but it worked better on all other, more important levels.

Alex could keep any adult absolutely busy thinking up games as he got to three, four, and five. Because I now had children two and worked more often, both Alex and Marina had to content themselves with surrogates some of the time. This they did quite happily, testing babysitters as to just how much they could manage. Marina went through a spate where I remember coming home several days to find her babysitter Julie's hair in many, small pigtails jutting straight out and up from her head. Seven or eight at least. Then there was Penelope, the lovely English girl who babysat for a bit when we first moved to London. The sight of Penelope in pearls, a stylishly up-turned collar and five blond pigtails jutting out from her head, one straight from her forehead like a unicorn, is burned into my memory bank forever. Finally, when Emma, a beautiful, lively sixteen-year-old English girl came to live with us, Marina moved into serious beauty training. Emma, after passing countless variations of the pigtail test, taught Marina to throw her head over and brush her hair from behind, which they did nightly, fifty strokes, along with many other mysteries of self-care initiated by Emma, who had been a stylish little girl not too long ago herself.

Alex managed to charm each and every babysitter we had into living out his fantasies. Jacquie he just loved and talked to and cuddled with and got her to swing him absolutely endlessly on the tires in the park. Mary read all his favorite books to him and let him sneak TV when I was out of the house. Martina he could get to be a horse or a cow or a cowgirl as he played all the other roles. She would also jump on the trampoline with him and play what he referred to as "wild games," lots of chasing and climbing and laughing. Agnes, the cellist from France, he discovered could paint. I came home one day to find that he had gotten her to turn his entire room into a forest by drawing trees with birds nesting and squirrels living in the knot on some large pieces of particle board that had been left over from a bit of construction. Some of these games would have to be played in pigtails if Marina was around. But it was Carmen, who didn't really know any good games, that I remember most guiltily. I wondered what he would get her up to. Then one quiet (too quiet) afternoon I walked by his room to see her gagged with his red, cowboy bandanna, and tied to one of his child chairs. In the absence of knowing a game, she became the game. Luckily she was having fun too. In on the joke she signaled me (with her eyes since her hands were tied . . . loosely, of course) that it was all in good fun.

Balancing Work and Mothering

The first thing to understand about balancing work and motherhood is that you will never get it right. You may always, off and on, feel conflicted about it, worried that your children will suffer, and then either selfish, tired, resentful, or occasionally relieved to get to work in order to get a rest. As long as you are having these feelings, don't worry, things will probably work out. You will put in the extra time to stay connected and attuned to your child and you will give up the extras in order to make that happen. If you aren't having them, if you find yourself telling people about how great your housekeeper is and how they have more patience than you and are probably better for your child than you are, then worry. You might be blocking important stuff, mainly the constantly nagging feeling that your kids really do need and miss you (and you really do need and miss them, maybe).

I stopped working full-time when I had Marina and it worked out better than I had thought it would on a lot of levels. I kept telling myself that I could have it all if I didn't have to have it all in the same decade. I could have family, a meaningful career, all of it, but maybe not all at once. Eventually, part-time allowed me to spend the kind of time I really felt pulled to spend with the children and still allowed me to maintain my career (which I also felt a big pull toward). It wasn't always the same; I worked much less when they were babies and toddlers and more as they grew up. I knew that it was a much easier matter to repair a neglected house than a neglected child. I had repaired too many as a therapist to be in any way confused on this point.

Developing Rapport

"Researchers . . . have tried to identify why some therapists seem to work magic on their clients. They have found that effective therapists tend to establish a rapport with clients by matching and pacing — in other words mirroring their tempo. The research suggests that matching and pacing another person has the effect of establishing rapport and increasing trust and openness" (Howard 2000). If you watch attuned mothers they do this naturally. They tune into their child's pace and rhythm. Children operate in their own time zone and mothers who are attuned are able to naturally tune into it. This makes communication flow much more naturally because the child is being met at the child's level. In this same way, the therapists who were studied in the research had this ability to tune in on where their clients actually are so that the client feels met and seen. Children need this meeting and seeing, too. They need to know we can feel our way into their world and be there with them.

When they were little, I just got down on the floor with them as soon as I came in the door after being gone. I feel like I spent years on the floor, but it was really the simplest way to reenter their world because that's where their world was happening. It was pretty easy to get on their wavelength because their wavelength was always somewhere in the back of my mind anyway. I would make eye contact, smell and touch my way back to them, and let them smell and touch their way back to me. As they got a bit older reconnecting took on many shapes, listening to what was on their minds, slowing down and settling into their rhythm for a few moments before launching into another activity, asking them about their day or finding out how something I knew they were doing had gone. Sometimes we would get dinner going together and they would take on some task that they wanted to do or they might keep me company while I started one.

I think I needed to reconnect as much as they did. Consciously reconnecting helped the rest of the day or evening to go much more smoothly. This walking in the door was an important moment, Mommy was coming home. I understood at some deep level not to take their love and need for me personally. All children love and need their mommies. A child's love is a gift from God that none of us earn.

Mommy was coming home. Not just me, Tian, but my children's mommy, the only one they had, the archetype that would live in their unconscious for life. I tried to be mindful of the gift of my children's love in my life and be aware that I could cause great wounds through it if I wasn't careful. There was such an inbuilt power imbalance in the relationship (that is, I had the power) and I wanted not to abuse that power. (Besides, I hoped that if I was nice to them when they were young and needed me maybe they'd be nice to me when I was old and needed them. So far, so good.)

Work travel was another kind of coming home. First of all, I tried to keep it to a reasonable amount, short and not too often. I organized everything ahead: Who would take care of them, special playmates and activities. Brandt actually liked getting me out of the way so that he could have his own relationship with the children for a few days. This helped a lot. He genuinely enjoyed my absence so the children felt that and at some level seemed to think it was fine. They, too, enjoyed having Daddy to themselves without me controlling, bossing, or otherwise insinuating myself all over the place. This was a real boon and made working so much more possible.

I, in turn, tried not to stretch anyone beyond their capacity. I didn't ask for more than was relatively easy to give and press my luck or take advantage. I tried to be available by phone but since most of my travel was for speaking engagements or to run workshops, I wasn't all that available. I picked and chose and did only the traveling that worked and left the other jobs for the next decade (or not). And I tried to schedule around important events (although as I write this I remember missing a couple of birthdays as they got older), This was a big deal and would require extra planning, substitute events, and so on.

I always brought presents. Always. They had to get something out of the deal. Marina and Alex seemed to take their cues from us. If we were okay with comings and goings, they seemed to feel that it was natural. If we felt conflicted, they picked up on that, too. As long as it wasn't too much, things went all right.

Women's Unique Response to Stress

According to a cutting- edge UCLA study, women have a range of response to stress that goes beyond fight-flight, freeze, to what researchers are calling tend and befriend. In stressful situations most men and women produce the hormone oxytocin, also known as the "touch chemical," the one that makes both people and animals "calmer, more social and less anxious," says the study's main researcher, Shelley E. Taylor. But that's where the similarity ends. The testosterone in men counteracts the calming effects of oxytocin while estrogen enhances it. Oxytocin can also lead to maternal behaviors, making women want to grab the children, gather with other women, and cluster for safety.

This research may turn some of our ideas about how stress affects men and women on its head and may also contribute to explaining why women live an average of seven and a half years longer than men. Oxytocin is a calming chemical that leads women to gather, talk, and support each other through stress while men tend to want to be alone in order to calm down from their unmitigated release of "stand and fight" stress hormones such as adrenaline. All of this was evolution's way of parceling out roles to maintain a tight "family of man" survival system.

It Takes a Village
Creating your mom support network

I do not believe in a child world...I believe the child should be taught from the very first that the whole world is his world, that adult and child share one world, that all the generations are needed. — Pearl S. Buck

Trains, planes, and automobiles have changed the fabric of American life. Historically, families have lived together out of economic need and communities rose up in close proximity because distances were hard to cross. But advances in transportation and technology have changed all that. It is a relatively recent phenomenon that families live so far apart. The "Village" that "it takes" to raise a child is on the run. The family system and the town that constituted our core "village" along with the relationships surrounding that core, like uncles, cousins, friends, co-workers, and faith institutions may no longer be at an easy arm's reach. So where do we find the village?

One thing a modern mother needs to get good at is creating her own support network. Even if you are lucky enough to be surrounded by relatives, having your own network is still a real source of sustenance. This can make all the difference in how you experience motherhood. Your support network can be very varied, but here are some basics to consider in both creating it and incorporating, into your day-to-day life:

Your Mom Friendship Network

This is the essential #1. Find other moms with kids roughly in the age range of your kids and form a loose play group or find park or playroom buddies. You can get together spontaneously (meet us in the park), weekly, bi-monthly, or monthly depending on need and availability. You can meet in a large group once a month and smaller, satellite groups more often. The kids can play and you can talk to each other about what it's like to be a mom, compare notes on child rearing and make plans to trade off babysitting so that you can get some free time during your week. Then your child will be left with a mom both of you know and a kid they can play with. Motherhood can be isolating, which can lead to depression, listlessness, and resentment. The mom friendship network is what can turn this around and make mothering feel communal and supported. The best time to start this is when you have an infant. Find another mom with an infant and build from there. Get together to talk about having a baby, then your network will be in place as your baby becomes a toddler.

Reach Out — Find Babysitting Help, Au Pairs, or Cleaning Help of Any Kind

Now's the time to have help if you can beg, barter, or buy it. The constant pick up and clean up involved in taking care of kids can be overwhelming. If you can, get some help.

Take Care of Your Body — If You Don't, Who Will?

Keep up your exercise and keep those endorphins, aka "feel-good body chemicals," flowing; you'll feel better. Find a gym that has babysitting, walk or jog in the park with a stroller and a friend who also has a stroller with a child in it. Or play in the back yard with your kids. We need to actively stimulate soothing and feel-good body chemicals and we do this through daily exercise. We also need our thirty minutes of sunlight a day so that we don't get down.

Families Who Play Together, Stay Together

Find other families to socialize with and entertain each other. It's easiest if one person provides the house and everyone else brings side dishes, desserts, etc. Picnics are great. Outings to movies and easy dinners or to theme parks are usually lots of fun. Make dinners kid friendly so that everyone will be happy. Eat on paper plates so clean up is not an issue. In my experience kids like good food, they don't need special menus if what's being served is kid friendly. Some families go camping with friends and kids usually love this sort of thing and renting cabins at the same place each year with friends or relatives can create wonderful, bonding experiences that last a lifetime.

Pay Attention to Your Heart

If motherhood is stimulating old issues from the past that are getting in the way of your being in the present, seek out extra help. I did this throughout raising Marina and Alex and am so grateful that I did; it helped me not to pass my stuff on to them. The benefit to them and to me was just enormous, and those benefits will be passed down to my grandchildren as well. I used my supports liberally and often at various points along my mothering in order to transform what was getting stimulated into growth, rather than act out and repeat pain. Some of these have been Alanon, one-to-one therapy, group therapy, faith-based counseling, couples therapy, and five-eight day programs for co-dependency.

Children literally absorb their mother's emotional world and it becomes a part of them. Because this is your child's only crack at childhood and because it is such a critical time in their development, you need to make your emotional wellness a priority. Though a painful past that is dogging your emotional trail may not be your *fault*, it is your *responsibility* to process and move through it. A depressed mother can leave a legacy of confusion and sadness in her child's heart. Our children need relatively happy parents to feel whole and well regulated emotionally. Get help if you need it. Now's the time.

Don't White-Knuckle It — Share Your Experience and Listen to Others

Find a support group for moms or start one. This can be one of the truly sustaining parts of your support network. Check *tiandayton.com* for suggestions on how to get a support group going and what to do once you've started it. Your support group can be incorporated into your moms' friendship network if you can work that out, but there is also an advantage in having a little separate time maybe even led by a professional if you can manage it.

Creating your own village is the only way I found to be a happy modern mother, as I was not living close to much extended family when my children were young, though we did lots and lots of visiting.

As your child grows, preschools and schools will also be a part of your village, but don't wait till then. You need other moms to talk to NOW. So start your informal gatherings — be proactive in this, for it will sustain you and will be your best source of information of every kind related to family needs.

Raising Ourselves

> *The mother-child relationship is, in a sense, tragic. It requires the most intense love on the mother's side, yet this very love must help the child grow away from the mother and become fully independent.* — Erich Fromm

A client of mine once described the less, well let's say, wonderful side of motherhood as "like waking up in the middle of the night with a flood in the house." Children take over everything, absolutely. Mothers sometimes experience a loss of self that can be difficult to get past. Being a mother can help us to build and strengthen a new sense of self but it can also wear us down and make us wonder who we are and what we are capable of.

One aspect of "role theory" which underlies psychodrama, a therapeutic role-playing method that I use in my practice, is that the self, rather than being some amorphous thing that arises out of who knows where, actually emerges from and is strengthened by the roles we play in our day-to-day lives. And these roles are set up *in relationship to others*, that is to say, they are co-created.

Kids Are Influenced by Their Parents' Emotions

"Clearly, the emotional state of others is of fundamental importance to the infant's emotional state," says Harvard child psychiatrist Edward Tronick. His choice of the word "others" rather than "mothers" is deliberate. Children form many important relationships with adults. A "mother" may be biological, adoptive, guardian, foster, grandparent, relative, friend. In recognizing the full range of emotional connection and intimacy, our society has begun to embrace a closer role for fathers as well. Infants may also scan a dad's face for comfort and for the kind of unconditional love that used to be seen as a mother's specialty. Babies send their parents nonverbal messages, too. Infants smile when they are pleased; cling when they need contact; follow with their eyes when they are worried that we may leave.

—T. Berry Brazelton and Bertrand G. Cramer, *The Earliest Relationship*

In this light, the loss of self that we naturally experience in early motherhood makes complete sense. It is part of adjusting to new roles and reducing some previous ones. So many of the roles we've been used to playing in our pre-children lives move straight into the background once we become mothers. Even though we may have been brilliant managers, competent, cool, and collected, two weeks of motherhood can have us babbling like idiots, feeling more inept and undertrained than we have felt in decades. And we haven't played our new mom related roles long enough to derive a sense of self or competence from them as yet. We feel unsteady, inept, and insecure. Our pre-mom sense of self may not help us much in this new role that demands a very different skill set from the one we have already developed. And the sense of self we used to derive from playing our pre-motherhood roles may be somewhat diminished simply because we're not playing them as much.

How Motherhood Transforms Us

New mothers are forced to find new ways of living and, to some degree, new roles and functions. In spite of the changes it is important to maintain the continuity of what you have known before. The result is a reshuffling in your mind, using the same cards that have been in play all along, your husband, your parents, siblings and extended family. This metamorphosis during the postpartum weeks, which is steeped in feelings of closing the past, almost always evokes a current of sadness merging with the larger river of joyful feelings. Assigning imagined identities and roles, especially to your baby, is one way of coping with the perceived losses.

The roles and identities you establish at this time set the direction for things to come. As a mother you are making a prophecy as to which people will be in your life and what they will mean to you, and these prophecies are self fulfilling. That is why it is so important to recognize this whole mental process. Your child and the rest of the family will have to live with the blueprints you design. They will become guidelines for the future, but because they usually are developed unconsciously they are rarely thought through with care. Do the guidelines really represent the future you want? — Daniel Stern, *The Birth of a Mother*

This can be especially tough for stay-at-home moms. All of the things we used to do we no longer do, and we spend the bulk of our time doing things we hardly know how to do. It's like being hired for an entry-level job with no training, no defined salary, no time off, no weekends, no lunch breaks, and, generally, little to no support staff. We just wake up one morning and life as we knew it is over. Our familiar markers are out of our line of vision and we don't know where to begin to find shore. The house is taken over and we, along with everything else, feel like we're underwater. Another factor that makes this transition even harder is the isolation that often accompanies being a new mom. More often than not our previous roles involved daily contact with others. So if we suddenly stop working, for example, all of that evaporates overnight with our first child, and the sense of community and structure we derived from it goes, too. This is why part of becoming a mom is to create a village in which to be one so we can build some of that community and camaraderie back into our days.

And here's some more good news. God never closes one door without opening another. Over time, if we keep at it, we will find something mysterious taking place. We will develop a fresh sense of self that will arise naturally out of playing our new mom roles. We will feel increasingly competent as we learn, day by day, to meet the challenges and resolve the issues that arise both past and present, as we take on this new role of mother and it's various sub-roles such as nurturer, listener, playmate, teacher, life planner, and coach. And all the competence and knowledge from our previous roles will still be with us. It's not lost, just shifted around. These are yet more ways that motherhood expands our foundation, our very self.

How Children Experience and Process Stress

Children do not have a fully developed capacity to understand what is happening around them and to regulate their intense emotional responses accordingly. That is why kids can get so excited or so scared. They depend upon the adults around them to help them to "contain" their excitement or "calm and soothe" their intense fear. The child's limited brain development can put them at risk if they are living in a chaotic environment, especially if the adults who they would normally go to for comfort are the source of the stress. Here's how that happens. "The amygdala, our fight/flight/freeze part of the brain, is fully formed at birth. This means that infants and children are capable of a *full blown stress response* from birth on. When frightened, their bodies will

go into fight/flight/freeze mode," says Dr. Shelly Aram of the Mead-
ows Treatment Center. That's why babies and toddlers can lose it
so fast or get so upset. And to complicate matters even further,
they don't have the brain development to assess what's going on
around them or understand why they are getting upset. That's because the hippocampus, or the part of the brain that interprets
sensory input as to whether or not it is a threat, is not fully func-
tional until between four and five years of age. So children have
no way of assessing whether or not they need to be scared and
how scared they need to be. They depend on us to help them
figure that out. And if that weren't enough, the prefrontal cortex,
which is where we have the ability to think and reason, is not
fully developed until around age eleven (Schore, *Affect Regulation and the Repair of the Self*). Therefore, when small children
get frightened and go into fight/flight/freeze, they "have neither
a way of interpreting the level of threat nor of using reason to
modulate or understand what is happening. Their limbic system
becomes frozen in a sensory fear response and can remain so,
without intervention from a caring adult, . . . and because of the
child's natural egocentricity the threat feels personal, it goes to
their core self" (Shelly Aram, lecture, April 2005), i.e., whatever
is going on, the child is likely to interpret as being "about them,"
they may feel they are the cause. Because they lack the developmental equipment to modulate this experience themselves, their
only way out of this state is through an external modulator, i.e.,
us . . . the parent, who can hold, reassure and restore them to
a state of equilibrium. If this modulating or cuddling them back
into a calm state occurs at the time of the upset, the child is
unlikely to become symptomatic because their parent is wooing
them back toward balance and a sense of safety. But if the parent
or family environment are the primary stressor and unavailable
to the child for reassurance, the child is left to live through repeated ruptures to his developing sense of self, his fundamental
learning processes and his relational world, with little ability to
make sense of it, interpret the level of threat or use reasoning
to regulate and understand what is going on. And later in life,
when that memory gets triggered, it is the same, unmodulated

sensory memory that was locked down to begin with. And they may still, as adults, be unconsciously living by the meaning they made as children, "I am bad, I cause trouble, I am at fault."

— Tian Dayton, *The Living Stage*

My Husband
Now the father of my children

Pains do not hold a marriage together. It is threads, hundreds of tiny threads which sew people together through the years. That's what makes a marriage last.

— Simone Signoret

After Marina was born, it was amazing how much less interesting Brandt became. Suddenly he seemed just too big. I was experiencing megatons of love vibrating out of a ten-pound body. Cuddling with Marina was an unparalleled experience that gave me extraordinary pleasure. Nursing her created an aura of contentment that fairly gave off physical warmth, and watching for her next smile was as riveting as I imagine panning for gold might be. You could have fried an egg on us. Who needed men? They were big and ate a lot and wanted the attention that I wanted to give exclusively to my daughter. I was in love, all right, but with Marina. Brandt, I now judged through a wholly different lens. How good a father is he? How much can he engage Marina? Does he love her as I do, with all his heart and another secret heart that he didn't know he had? Would he do for her, fetch, carry, would he die for her? Because I knew I would. I was much more interested in Brandt as a father to Marina than as my husband. His abilities as a father became a key element in how I evaluated him as my mate.

How the Self Emerges from the Roles We Play

Thinking, feeling, and behavior tend to be role-specific, that is, we think, feel, and behave in ways appropriate to the role we are playing. A mom thinks like a mom, feels the emotions that being a mom arouses, and does the things moms do. The role is the tangible form the self takes and the self emerges and gets its shape from the roles we play (Moreno 1946). Well-adjusted people tend to play a variety of roles, for example, mother, wife, worker, exerciser, friend, sister, daughter, etc. When we can experience a balance of roles in our lives, moving in and out of them with ease and fluidity, we guard against feeling burnt out, depressed, or stuck. Each stage in life has its own constellation of roles. When we move from one stage to the next, we add some roles and modify others. Looking at life changes in terms of role shifts can help us to make these changes with greater optimism and intelligence.

And when Alex came along it happened all over again and was even more difficult because now he had to be a good father to a boy. I felt more confident that I could fill in, if there were missing pieces, with a girl. But with a boy, I didn't. I felt that Alex needed a father to model who could show him how to be a man. And suddenly I wanted Brandt to be a perfect man to model for our son. Perfectly. Flawlessly. Every fault Brandt had stood out to me in high relief and I wanted him to get over it, get past it, right it. I wanted him to be what I could never be. The right man for Alex. "Scientists can point to animal communities where this is true as well. A female baboon with a baby will allow a male into her life only if he proves himself a good caregiver to the youngster" (Stern 1998). Luckily, Brandt was so sweet with Marina and Alex that I found myself falling in love with him all over again as their father. This, however, didn't stop my critiquing him in my head.

Stress in the Body

The body can't tell the difference between an emotional emergency and physical danger. When triggered, it will respond to either by pumping out stress chemicals designed to impel someone to quick safety or enable them to stand and fight. In the case of childhood problems where the family itself has become the proverbial saber-toothed tiger, there may be no opportunity to fight or flee. Children in these families may find escape impossible. And so they do what they can. They freeze. They shut down their inner responses by numbing or fleeing on the inside. Though this strategy may have helped them to get through a painful situation, perhaps for a period of many years, they suffered within. The ability to "escape" or take one's self out of harm's way is central to whether or not one develops long term trauma symptoms or PTSD (Van der Kolk 1987). If escape is not possible, the intense energy that has been revved up in the body to enable fight or flight becomes thwarted or frozen (Levine 1997). Years later these people may live as if the stressor is still present, as if a repeated rupture to their sense of self and their world lurks just around the corner, because their body/mind tells them it does. This is part of why early childhood pain can have long-lasting effects.

But still, since the kids came first he, in my mind, had to learn how to come second. I was coming second and had mixed feelings about it. Part of it was shocking and shoved my own life, identity, and sense of self into the background. I resented being the one who so much of the work fell on. And part of it was freeing, somehow, not to be constantly preoccupied with me, to have a vacation from my own life and worrying if it was going the way it should. I had an instant sense of mission and purpose. Motherhood. I was in a long line of the female of every species that had ever walked this earth. Birds, squirrels, monkeys, lions, and puppies. All of us, the same at some profound, biological level. Here to nurture our young and make sure they get off to the right kind of start. It was hard for me to balance our needs as a couple alongside our children's needs. I don't think I did it all that well. I'm glad our marriage survived. I think it helped that we all developed a strong identity as a family that we were equally invested in.

At the same time as I was judging Brandt within an inch of his life I also felt uncomfortably dependent upon him. What if he left? What if he abandoned us huddling under some tree (in the very middle of a snowstorm or a hurricane)? I felt a kind of vulnerability I had never felt in my life. That I really couldn't do this alone and that he was connected to me in a much more profound way than previously. What if it didn't work? Until now I had always had the sense that I could take care of myself. Now I wasn't so sure. It took everything I had and then some just to take care of Marina and eventually Alex. I was at my absolute limit and I needed Brandt as never before to be Marina's and Alex's father, provider, and attention giver. This felt like a tall order and I only hoped we were both up to it. Our relationship, just like each of us as individuals, became less central, too. In a way it was sort of nice not to worry about "us" for a change and worry about "them" instead. To make the little slings and arrows that were so preoccupying to us, all the little nuances of our togetherness which had been so unbearably crucial that we get right, less important. Though eventually we did have to vigorously address our issues so they didn't leak all over the children.

Being an adult child of an alcoholic (ACOA) who learned, at a young age, to be self-reliant, I think I found feelings of dependency especially hard. They just aroused too much anxiety. Eventually, I got into therapy to explore that and other things, but I think it would have been helpful to me, at the time, to formulate the right questions so that I didn't layer my anxiety onto the wrong place (namely, Brandt and the children). I would have liked to be able to ask myself questions like, What does attachment, with all its feelings of dependence, yearning, need, and vulnerability, bring up for me from my own history, my own early experiences of attachment? How might I be projecting all of this into my current relationship with my husband or my child? Or into the middle of the triangles formed by us and each of our children? Or how might he be projecting his early experiences onto me? How can I separate the past from the present so the present doesn't become any more overwhelming than it already is? How can I marshal all the wonderful gifts and strengths I gained in childhood and use them here while at the same time squarely facing my complexes and anxieties and working with them so they don't trickle out in the all the wrong ways?

These feelings of attachment, with all their power to awaken the fears, insecurities, and strengths lying dormant inside of me, were the gift, the Theseus thread that, if I followed it through the labyrinth of my own heart and mind, could lead me to freedom.

Our Undying Need to Love

> *Learning from their children is the best opportunity most*
> *people have to assure a meaningful old age.*
> — M. Scott Peck

In the 1950s, a psychologist named Harry Harlow wanted to "study love" and infant attachment to the mother. In order to do this he created "surrogate mothers" from tubes of cylindrical meshed wire. He wrapped a piece of Turkish towel around one of the "mothers" and left the other one only wire mesh. The "wire mother" had a bottle strapped to her body from which a baby monkey could drink milk and just a suggestion of a face, while the "cloth mother" wore a sort of gawky, gray/green paper monkey face with huge, round eyes. The infant monkeys tended to spend most of their time clinging to the cloth mother. Though they got no food from her, they received the sensation of touch and searched her paper face for signals of relatedness. This "touching" along with their apparent instinct to bond to a mother's face was more important to them than food. It was emotional food that created calm feelings. It released the oxytocin that made them feel good and also released brain fertilizers that they needed for healthy growth.

On the Children in Romanian Orphanages

Scientific study confirmed what the untrained eye could see: The children were in the third to tenth percentile for physical growth, and "grossly delayed" in motor and mental development, Carlson says. They rocked and grasped themselves like Harlow's monkeys, and grew up with weird social values and behavior. As they aged, many of the orphans became homeless, with "clumsy, sad, all inappropriate" social interactions. To express affection, one boy might kiss another on top of the head. Smiling and ingratiating, the youths are superficially friendly but unable to form permanent attachments. Like characters in a gloomy sci-fi novel, many found work in the secret police where their lack of loyalty and ability to make "friends" were salable.

Chemical analysis also showed abnormal cortical profiles. The children who were raised with maternal deprivation had overly sensitized stress responses. They were constantly revved up for fight-flight. Being able to run or fight when necessary is adaptive and a critical survival skill. However, when our early environments are depriving and thus highly stressful we become permanently sensitized to stress throughout life.

They went to the wire mother who had the food only when hungry, then they returned to the comfort of the soft cloth and the gaping paper face. For every one hour they spent with the wire mother, they spent seventeen hours with the cloth mother in order to receive this sensation related to touching and cling-ing. Even after a six-month separation from their "mother," these baby monkeys, when exposed to scary stimuli, leapt onto their cloth mothers, clinging for their lives. The infant's need to attach to a mother is so powerful that in the absence of a real, warm body, even a towel wrapped around a cylinder of wire that allows them to self-stimulate will do. It should be noted, however, that these baby monkeys grew up to have sig-nificant and long-lasting problems that evidenced themselves in symptoms of acute anxiety, a lack of ability to relate well, and unusual aggression and withdrawal.

Crossing the street once, hand in hand, Marina asked me, "Do parents love their children the way children love their parents?" Shocked at the question I replied, "Yes, of course, mothers would do anything for their children, there is no one more important than you to me." Inside I was wondering if I had in some way failed to communicate my love or if she was just being her questioning, penetrating self. "Don't you feel how much I love you, Marina?" "Yes, I was just wondering, because children always love their parents, always."

I realize now that she was speaking to the inborn need of a child to love and depend. She was aware that this was just a part of being a child. Oh, Marina. Deep little girl. "All chil-dren always love their parents." What a responsibility we have, I thought, not to fail these little people who look to us for so much. But I also realized that love is cumulative. Crossing the street hand in hand, combing her hair, making her lunches, touching, tucking her in, listening to her thoughts, reading to-gether, cooking together, running an errand that becomes a moment of exploration and togetherness . . . just being in each other's worlds, looking, seeing, being . . . this is love. How it builds and fills the space in between us with a secure sort of glow. How we wear it on each of our faces and carry it in each of our hearts. How it is part of our thoughts and our feelings and our bodies. This is the kind of love mothers and children share. This bond that allows a woman to pick up a tractor to get her trapped daughter out from underneath or run into traffic without a thought to rescue a wandering son or give up pieces of herself to sustain her children. This superhuman but oh so very human kind of love. I experience God in your presence, little girl, and in your brother's. Bliss. Love like I have never known before, that is daily shaping me into a new and better person. "Yes, Marina, parents love their children just as much as children love their parents. Thank you for wondering."

How Not to Pass on Pain

If there is anything we wish to change in the child, we should first examine it and see whether it is not something that could better be changed in ourselves.

—Carl Jung

Our feelings can follow unusual, circuitous paths, they can play hide and seek with us. One of Marina's favorite things to do when she was two and three was to visit Gramma at her big and beautiful apartment on Fifth Avenue. She loved the mirrors on the doors where she could watch her face moving through any and every sort of expression; Gramma's cook, Marie, who made her artichokes and hollandaise; and all the pretty things Gramma had to look at. She followed Gramma around, as they carefully lifted up and admired her little Limoges boxes. And across the street in Central Park was a pony ride and a Child's Clock Tower where a monkey struck the hour and storybook animals rotated around the clock to music. She and eventually Alex loved it. We visited Gramma from our house in the foothills of the Poconos about every five or six weeks. The contrast was not lost on Marina. Even at three, she recognized all of the rarified pleasures and intrigue of a big, sophisticated city. And she loved being at Gramma's and soaking up her surroundings, an elegant, pastel world where everything was shined, framed, and tastefully laid out. A Virgo's paradise.

Imaginary Friends — Emotions Can Be Elusive:
The Many Ways We Hide Our Feelings

Generally transitions were no issue. Marina was happy to go and happy to return to our simple country life with two dogs and lots of outdoors. But I recall returning from New York after one of our visits and Marina was unusually out of sorts. Her mood was generally very cheery so I was concerned that she was coming down with something. All day I asked her questions designed to find out what was bothering her only to be frustrated at every turn. I couldn't figure out what was wrong so I couldn't help her feel better. Late in the afternoon, wracking my brain as to how to discover the source of her uncharacteristic ill temper I tried as a final attempt to expand my search. Marina had an imaginary friend named "Cha-cha."

"How's Cha-cha, Marina?" I asked. Marina swung her head around and fixed on me with her does like eyes.

"Cha-cha moved."

"Cha-cha moved?" I queried back-sensing I was finally getting somewhere.

"Cha-cha moved at New York!" said Marina, locking me into a gaze that had all the piercing intensity of a Sensei (or something) master.

She had nailed it, named the problem and, on a symbolic level, concretized the issue. Cha-cha (read Marina) did not want to be here in this boring, backwater place with no horsy ride, no hollandaise, and no Gramma. Cha-cha had chosen New York, thank you very much.

"Do you wish we were still in New York, Marina?" Marina's face softened as emotion filled it. Tears came into the corners of her big, hazel eyes.

"I miss Gramma's."

Once Marina had named this, owned it and felt the feeling of missing consciously, she didn't even need to talk about it further. Her mood shifted immediately. She was back to normal.

Our emotions do not necessarily follow a predictable, linear path. Sometimes we have to search for them, knock on closed doors, mine our dreams for meaning, and interpret emotional responses or physical aches and pains in order to learn what's going on. Cha-cha, for example, knew the feeling that was keeping Marina feeling moody for no apparent reason. The mind is a complex place.

The Power of Unconscious Memories — Marina's Powder-Blue Coat

Marina was born in September so she spent her first winter in my arms where I knew I could keep her safe and warm. The next winter was another story. She was on her own feet and as winter started to approach, I became obsessed with finding her a blue, wool coat, hat, and muff to guard her against the cold. I looked everywhere from Bergdorf's to Sear's catalogue and everything in between. But try as I did, it seems that little coats and muffs were a relic of the fifties and even fancy little baby stores weren't reviving them (in her size) in the late seventies, the days of mod chic or one size fits all. I somehow couldn't feel satisfied that Marina would be warm and comfortable in anything other than a little wool ensemble. One in which she could snuggle down, twirl rabbit fur in her fingers, rub it up against her face, smell it and fall asleep in a secure little foxhole of fur and mothballs.

Desperate to outfit her with what I felt was the only thing that would work to keep her warm and snug, I hunted around for a seamstress, bought powder-blue wool (and pink for next year) and had a coat, hat, and muff made. Even though I couldn't quite use real rabbit's fur, I told myself she would be happy with it, mostly. When we visited my mother in Florida, Marina wore her coat to the airport. As I was unpacking, I showed it to my mom, who commented that she hadn't seen them around for a long time, that they weren't the thing everyone wore as they had been when she raised her children.

Tian: "Did I have one?"

Mom: "Yes, you loved it. You used to cuddle up in it; we almost lost you inside of it."

Tian: "What color was mine?"

Mom: "You had a powder-blue one and a pink one. The powder-blue was your favorite."

I was stunned at the power of the unconscious to remember what the conscious mind had forgotten. I simply couldn't let go of the idea that Marina had to have this little outfit that had given me so much pleasure as a child, that I remember sinking into like a turtle in a shell, with only my eyes remaining above sea level. I translated that into a worry that she wouldn't be comfortable without it and an obsession to find, in any way possible, what I "knew" she had to have. All this with absolutely no conscious awareness as to the origins of the perceived need, the source of the wish.

I write this to illustrate the power of the unconscious mind to influence our thinking, feeling, and behavior without our knowing it. I had no idea that the reason I was so convinced Marina couldn't face winter without a blue coat and muff was because of my own childhood experience. Our childhood experiences lie dormant in our unconscious and become stimulated when we have our own children. But we're seldom aware of the why or the wherefore. The experiences we had as children get "warmed up" when we reenter an environment that compares with our childhood experience, namely raising our own children and having our own intimate relationships. We bring the family we were raised in into the family we raise.

How Emotional Pain Gets Passed Down
through the Generations

There is something called an "age correspondence reaction," illustrated by the story of Marina's blue coat and the following one about Alex. It means that when our children reach a particular age they trigger, in us, what was going on in our lives at that same age. Wow. Thank God I've had that bit of knowledge. Understanding the dynamics of the age correspondence reaction is, I think, one of the keys to growing from parenting. It's what allows us to recover rather than repeat.

When Alex was in seventh grade I became convinced that he was having a difficult year. (I probably did the same thing with Marina, as I look back, but because she'd been elected president of the middle school I could ward it off; I probably needed her super success just to feel normal. But she changed schools after that year so my complex may — duh — have been internalized by her with no awareness on my part.)

So here's the story. In spite of all evidence to the contrary, I was worried. I was convinced that Alex was having a hard year but even I had brains enough to realize that I should check out my perception — as Mark Twain said, "You can't necessarily trust your eyes if your mind is out of focus." By now I knew, thanks to therapy and Alanon, that my mind could be out of focus. So I called the school, who said that he was having not only a good but a terrific year, and I asked some mom friends who knew him and they all said he seemed great, and I called his pediatrician, who told me it was probably me, that he seemed fine.

I decided to do something we call a social atom in psychodrama (a sort of relationship diagram). I did an atom of my life in seventh grade during the fall months. To my utter amazement I got the picture immediately. When I was in seventh grade, my parents took us, as a family, to Greece to live for a year to "learn about who we are" as they said. For the first three months I was miserable: I had no friends and I missed my friends from Northrup terribly, especially my best friends, Anne and Suzie. After I adjusted I never wanted to come back, because I loved it so much and made so many new friends. It was this friend thing that should have been the tip-off. I was worried daily that Alex didn't have enough friends against daily evidence to the contrary. He brought friends home all the time and was constantly getting together with them, and his teacher reported that he was among the most well liked, popular kids in his class. All of this evidence didn't take away my anxious feelings until I *made the connection with that time in my own life*. A classic age correspondence reaction, my problems at that age were triggered and layered mindlessly onto his life when he became a similar age. Marina's powder-blue coat all over again but in a new guise. When Marina was in seventh grade, she actually wound up applying to and changing schools by eighth (as I had). Luckily changing schools had been in the plan anyway, just a year later. Wow. The mind is a terrible thing (period, not even to waste, just period, all by itself; eeks!).

These unconscious dynamics never cease to amaze me. That our behavior can be so unconsciously driven speaks to the complex ability of the mind to retain emotional, sense, and behavioral impressions from the past and recreate them in the present. The bonds that form the core of our early relationships really do form a template or map for subsequent relationships throughout our lives. The pain we can't move past in some way repeats itself in our parenting. We project our unhealed pain unto our children, all too often. Our problems with our mother or father become our problems with our daughter, son, or spouse. Our own unhealed issues from our family of origin can leak out into the emotional atmosphere of our family today.

Recycled pain locks us and our children into repeating, hurt-filled dynamics that spread unhealed wounds through the generations. One of the greatest gifts we can give our children is to finish off our unfinished business so that it doesn't get passed along. Motherhood gives us a chance to heal it instead of pass it down through yet another generation. But, in order to heal it, we need to reach out when we are overwhelmed and lost. We need to recognize that we can't, nor should we try to, do it alone. We need to learn to ask for help, to extend and use our village.

Motherhood is paradoxical. It requires us to *enter into* our children's world in order to understand them, but if we *become* our children's inner world and lose our own identity this can lead to problems. We need to have our own sense of self and allow children to have theirs so that we don't mix our issues up with their inner world creating a tangle that snags each of us. We need to learn how to enter their world, and still retain our own sense of self and let them retain theirs. Again, this requires cleaning up our own issues both past and present. Separating our pain from our children's and historical "hysterical" over-reactions in the present that have their roots in the past is part of being a good parent.

———=«(●)»=———

There is only one corner of the universe
that you can be certain of improving . . .
and that's yourself. — Aldous Huxley

———=«(●)»=———

If we want to raise emotionally literate children, we need to become emotionally literate adults. Excess emotional baggage and unfinished business from the past make emotional literacy very tough to attain and maintain. This is because emotional literacy requires that we first have the ability to sit with what is going on inside of us. It also asks that we can tolerate the strong emotions that get aroused in us when we are in intimate connection with another person. If we can't tune in our own inner world in order to better understand it, or listen to some-one else express what might be going on in theirs, emotional literacy will elude us. Because all of this emotional languag-ing is a fairly recent phenomenon, some people have simply never learned to experience, name, process, and talk about their feelings. If this is the case, practice will make perfect, you can learn it. Some of us learn it in therapy, support groups, or groups that talk in an emotional language, i.e., not generally at work or in a reading group. One of the other common reasons that people have trouble "sitting with" the intensity of their own inner worlds is because they contain unresolved pain and re-sentment from past relationships. If we don't pay attention to resolving these inner conflicts they are bound to resurface in our current relationships. Finishing up our unfinished business to keep it from leaking into the pores of another generation is a very significant legacy that we can leave our children and grandchildren. It is money in their emotional and psychological banks from which they and their children will draw interest for literally lifetimes. An emotional trust fund. Otherwise, more often than not they will have to assume our emotional debts. They will inherit our baggage.

If early relationships were painful, we may blame ourselves in the secret corners of our hearts. We weren't good enough, pretty enough, smart enough. And when that pain hurts too much to feel, we want to get rid of it by projecting it outward onto someone else. We make it about them and not us. Working through our unfinished business is important for our children so that our unspoken shame and pain doesn't become theirs.

Processing emotional pain and working toward acceptable resolution and even forgiveness is a process, not an event. It happens in layers. It is blocked by anger, resentment, and hurt. All of this is what we need to confront and work through so that our emotional work can be genuine. Resolution and forgiveness that are only lip service simply drive pain into a deeper place, twist it into another shape. C. S. Lewis said that "it takes two to see one." We do not need to do this alone. Trying to deal with the deep, unresolved pain from family-of-origin issues, for example, generally requires the support and insight of others to help us tolerate the pain and see the meaning we have made out of our past that we may still be living by today. When we have been hurt as children we often erect powerful defenses to keep pain out. To keep people and intimacy out. To keep deep feeling and connection out. We may deny, repress, or twist our pain around into another, more acceptable shape rather than feel and process it. This, of course, weakens our ability to be emotionally literate because as soon as we have an emotion we don't want to have, we numb it out or project it onto someone else. We lose touch with ourselves and complicate our relationships when we do this. We have a thousand ways of distancing them such as stonewalling, withdrawing, or engaging in constant anger, irritation, or criticism. Even enmeshing identities is a way of distancing because it denies each person the circle of safety around themselves in which they can experience themselves. And then we start to feel suffocated, we withdraw, fight, or disappear in order to gain some breathing room, some emotional space. The emotional worlds of parents and children are constantly overlapping and they need to for the child to thrive. So when our emotional worlds are filled with conflicts and unresolved, painful emotions that keep us from having a healthy self, this overlapping of worlds means that the children absorb it and may even incorporate it into themselves as if it were theirs without awareness that this unconscious process has occurred. Because children really do want to come in, they bang on the door of our hearts until they can get them to open, until their little fists turn black and blue. And if they can't get in and find us, they often feel inadequate. So healing our wounds from the past allows us to keep old pain from spilling over into our relationships with our children and partners in the present. And it opens those emotional doors that allow us to feel more fully, so that we don't have to block the intensity of our children's neediness and love because it triggers our own. What happens in our family of origin gets recreated through our parenting because that's the way brain and memory work. What we learned as children may lie dormant for many years. But when we're in a situation that is similar, i.e., another family, all that learning resurfaces and gets played out on a new stage, the stage of our own families. Our children stimulate the child in us.

For years my motto was Oscar Wilde's famous "living well is the best revenge." I knew that getting back at someone else by ruining my own life through self-destructive behavior was a fool's revenge. I would only hurt myself, my husband, and my children. I'd ruin my own life and everything that matters to me. Today I have added onto that another adage, "forgiveness is the best revenge." When we decide to forgive, we are challenging ourselves to work through all of the problematic emotions that block forgiveness like anger, resentment, and hurt. We are choosing freedom from emotional, psychological, and spiritual bondage. And we are leaving someone else's bad behavior, and for that matter our own, with them where it belongs. We are working through the residue of less-than-optimal experiences and bringing them into light and understanding, growing from adversity rather than living in it. And we are disentangling ourselves from the kind of back and forth, tit for tat, that will only keep us down, that will spread toxic waste into the healthy environment we wish to create and live in today.

Healing my own family-of-origin relationships as much as possible has been the most helpful way of lifting this dynamic. And even if I can't heal them fully with a person who may no longer be with us or not be interested, I can heal the part of the pain that lives in me. I can heal and move on. Being open to change and love and new types of relating has really been wonderful.

Prayer and Projecting the Positive

As much as 80 percent of adult success comes from EQ.
— Daniel Goleman

The power of prayer is one of the very real blessings on the path of motherhood.

I find prayer, going within, and visioning to oftentimes be very effective in changing behavior in myself and my children or moving circumstances along for the better. When I am concerned about my children, I always try to remember to try prayer, going within, and visioning. I lie on my bed, generally, or sit in a quiet place and go within. I rest in a connection with God. I like to use the mind's natural imaging. I imagine Alex, Marina, or myself or Brandt to be happy, whole, and productive. I hold this image for a moment and release it and continue to do this over and over again throughout the day. If there is a circumstance in any of our lives that is not going well, I picture it improving. I find that it is important to connect with source energy and align my will with God's will for all concerned. Because prayer is so powerful, it is possible, in my experience, to get what you pray for. And so often we pray for the immediate gratification without seeing the big picture. So I find that praying for what is right for all concerned, over time, produces sounder, happier results.

Praying also gives me tremendous relief. It elevates my mind and moves something I'm worrying about into a more positive place. I pray to learn, too. That the children will learn from whatever they are going through, be strengthened, see more clearly. I pray for a shift in perception that will allow me to see a situation in its most spiritual, positive light. Not positive in the sense of denying and rewriting reality so that I can better live with it, which makes everyone around me feel crazy and nullified, but positive in the sense that good will ultimately prevail and that we will learn and grow toward light and wisdom.

Most of us as parents turn to prayer and if you haven't yet, I highly recommend it. Prayer has been one of the best ways for me to deal with my anxiety as a parent. If I can turn my children over to a benevolent Higher Power, place them and all of us in the loving arms of God, I feel less lonely and anxious. Psychologists have long known that talking about anxiety relieves it because we use our words to concretize these nagging fears and worries and communicate them, and they lessen as we talk them through. Prayer is a process of bringing these worries to a conscious level and communicating them, too. We communicate them to our creator and look to the Spirit to work with us in resolving them, dissolving them, or living with them differently. I pray about anything and everything, nothing is too small or big. Marina's desk, Alex's play, their play dates, my work life, their friends, their eventual partners, their school experience, you name it. And I truly believe that prayer often helps all of us more than other things I might do, and that prayer is an action that will benefit them in unseen ways. I have witnessed this more times than I can count. So prayer is more than it appears: hardly a solitary act, it has transformative power, it moves into the ether, like radio waves, and vibrates at the right pitch to enter the ear of God — to unite with the creative life forces that are always surrounding us.

As a mother I worried about lots of things. I worried about my own adequacy as a mother, would I have what it took to make it through the long haul? Did I have the resources on all levels to meet the moment adequately? I worried about the children's friendships. Did they have good friends, were they popular, did they suffer rejection? I worried about how they felt in school. Did they feel smart enough, were they anxious, did their teachers like them, were they good to them? I had separate worries for each of them, of course, and the worries changed over time, but I worried too much. I think part of it was because raising children in today's world when we're all super aware of what can go wrong adds a layer of anxiety. I also think part of it was because my father's alcoholism and my mother's preoccupation with keeping things going and not looking at anything too closely left me emotionally alone too much of the time. Some of my own unfinished business got mixed up with my children's very normal struggles. At some unconscious level, the child inside of me who still needed healing got projected onto my kids. Unconsciously I was still caught in another time and place, living in an emotional world from yesterday that kept getting mixed up with today. The amount of therapy and Alanon I did to clear out my own issues staggers the imagination. But I needed all of it to turn the tide of addiction, relationship trauma, divorce, and the accompanying dysfunction that were dogging my emotional trail. I did what I felt I had to do, I "worked it till it worked." And there is not a day that goes by when I am not unbelievably grateful that I did.

Prayer and visualization helped me to manage this and other more ordinary kinds of anxiety. I used it as a sort of antidote to my own negative thinking. I would lie in my bed, go into a calm state, and lift my energy. I'd picture my children and our family whole, happy, and thriving. I would see them in my mind's eye as free of needless concern and in a good and positive frame of mind. I'd see them with good relationships and succeeding in their endeavors. I always felt that at the very least this was better for them than my unconscious, negative forecasting. In addition to disciplining myself to project positive rather than negative images, this was my attempt to lift my own pain off of them, so to speak, to make the part of me conscious that was seeing things in a negative light and turn it around. Because I knew they felt it.

The Power of Prayer

Prayer has as profound a beneficial effect on depression as drugs do. Over and over again, studies prove this, according to Larry Dossey, M.D., author of *Healing Words*. Praying to God actually elevates the immune system. The same kinds of body chemicals that are present in the mother/child connection are present when we pray. Spiritual connection, it seems, is something akin to an intimate experience of touching and being touched. Larry Dossey says that the research on the power of prayer to shrink malignant tumors is so convincing that if it could be bottled, drug companies would be making billions on it.

We all visualize all the time; it is a natural activity or function of our minds. When we worry about our children excessively we are surrounding them with our anxious images, and these images get communicated to them on a subliminal level; they feel them, they take them on. Sometimes it is appropriate to be anxious and it can be even helpful for kids to pick up on what makes us worry so that they can adjust their own behavior. But the kind of anxiety that emerges out of our unresolved issues from the past or our own unsatisfied selves actually burdens our children and gets in their way. Our issues get carried by their unconscious. They may pick up on our pain and take it on as their own as a way of making sense of it. It floats around the atmosphere, becomes mixed up with the subtleties and va-garies of family life. It gets pinned in all the wrong places. This is why one of the greatest gifts that we can give our children is to resolve our own stuff before we pass it onto them. It is also why consciously imaging them in positive ways makes us aware of the amount of time we spend doing just the opposite.

Choosing Life

We are not trying to educate children and send them into the world as finished products — we are working to send them forward as people well begun.   —Sr. Angela Bayo

If I have learned one thing, it is that love and relationship is at the center of everything. Having my own children was, for me, a second chance at living. A window into a world I thought I'd left behind forever or even lost. A golden opportunity to make cupcakes important and to get excited all week about a red truck. The endless memories of Alex climbing anything and everything and waving to me from the top of it or the feeling of his three-year-old legs like a vice around my waist are what are mine to keep forever, even though he has long since become a man. And the sight of Marina quietly engaged in one of her many industrious projects, humming to herself, making magic bars for her endless bake sales, enjoying her lovely companionship or the tenderness of her forgiving arms, that is what children can give you that no one else can; pieces of yourself you thought you'd lost, suddenly there. The imprint of their child bodies against my own, the scent of them and the pleasure of mothering them is still and always with me.

It is a spiritual gift to know that you are going to die some-day. Because until you do, you don't really understand how to value life. I received this gift when I was thirty-five; well in time for it to do some good. I knew that my time with Marina and Alex in my home was limited, as are all experiences. I understood that if I didn't make use of the time I had with them, I would not get it back. It would simply be gone and I would have to live with knowing that I had wasted it. I also knew what it meant to lose a home, to have it disappear before your very eyes and suffer that pain for years and years. I knew that what I had was precious and limited. I resolved, not even consciously but through the overwhelming experience of having illness knock at my door and then fly away, to live the life I really wanted to live rather than the one I thought I was supposed to live. I had a mission, to raise my children as well as I was capable of, to clean out my own emotional closet before it cleaned me out, and to search for the real meaning of life using the experience of motherhood that God was putting before me as one of my important stimuli and vehicles for soul growth. Right at the end of my arm were all the daily lessons that reveal the mysteries of the universe, the purpose of living, and the meaning of life, if I could learn to look properly. If I could surrender to the experience.

The Spiritual Work of Healing the Self

I really think that Christianity as well as some other faiths were given to us as a method to heal the self in order to grow spiritually, to teach us that it is through the vehicle of self-examination that we do, in fact, grow closer to God. The Bible talks to us in allegorical forms about inner transformation. On the cross some of Christ's final words were "forgive them, God, for they know not what they do." All along we are receiving words that, if we follow them, liberate us. "Do onto others as you would have others do unto you." These two concepts, forgiveness and mindful action, seem to me to be about liberating my own spirit from the mindless repetition of pain, of being marooned forever on the wheel of karmic-like cycles.

I think motherhood has been one of the most significant places that I have put these principles into action. My love for my children is the closest thing to selfless love that I've ever known. I think it was years of this that got me out of myself long enough to understand that it really is in giving that we receive and in dying to the small self that we are born into the higher self. By selfless action, I don't mean not taking care of myself; motherhood has driven that point home. I need to give to myself with the same charitable and loving hand that I give to them, for their sake even if not for mine. If I can't love myself then how can I love them? So giving to myself in this spiritual context isn't any more selfish or unselfish than giving to them. We are all God's children. God gave my children to me to take care of and God gave me to me to take care of. Life is a gift and it is my responsibility to value it and live it as well as I can. To make the most of all I have been so generously given. When I treat my children as I would wish to be treated, when I take good care of all of us, I am sowing high-quality seeds for me, for them, for my grandchildren and for the world.

And more times than not, charitable action toward them also necessitates the same toward myself and other family members because conflicts are so often co-created. Even if we're not the aggressor, we may have a piece in creating a problem, however big or small. This intergenerational right-minded action, prayer, and forgiveness frees generations past, present, and future. It wasn't until after years of practicing these attitudes with my children that I tried them with my husband. And they work there too. I think I confused them with not being able to stand up for myself or being a doormat. But it's not like that. It's been my children that have taught me to step back and stretch. In not wanting to hurt them, I've wound up not hurting myself; in forgiving them, I've wound up forgiving myself and others; and in treating them as I would like to be treated, I've elevated my own emotional and spiritual standard of living.

And motherhood has helped me to appreciate that a big part of being a good mother is to learn to find balance in my own life. A child doesn't only grow up with a mother. She grows up in the atmosphere of the home and marriage and its extension into aunts, uncles, cousins, grandparents, friends, schools, and the neighborhood that she lives in. All of this is what our children take in day after day, upon which they build their sense of themselves and the world in which they live. A happy mother goes a very long way, and a happy home, balanced with friends and extended family, school, work, social life, errands, and so forth blend together to form the child's early world. The way they are allowed to operate in this world teaches them a lot about how to be in a relational context. It is the microcosm of the world they will inhabit as adults.

Science only sees what the person behind the scientific investigation is capable of conceiving. It is a hopeful thing, then, cause for celebration that science now "reveals" what good mothers have known for centuries. That mothering is an interactive process between mother and child where each party impacts, shapes, and transforms the other. This is why motherhood is a spiritual path. It has the power to transform us from within, to reach into the most alive parts of us and call us to our real natures. We are doing God's work as mothers. Each morning when I woke up with Marina and Alex in our home, I felt an excitement. God and I had work to do. And the work was immediate, involving, and spiritual in nature. Because we were people making. What could be more important? And what more significant contribution can we as mothers make to all of our worlds than people "well begun"? As George Vaillant says, "generativity flows downward," our best shot at having a rich and ripe old age is to care about, support, and love the generations beneath us.

People Well Begun

Mothering wasn't much respected in the late seventies and early eighties. Accomplishment was center stage. But I couldn't help feeling that if I didn't accomplish this all-important task, nothing else I might do would matter much. So I rebalanced my life to make my children center stage. It's not that I gave up my own dreams, profession, and passions, but I tried to incorporate my kids into my social world and arrange my life so that their lives didn't get "back-burnered." There was no one out there in the world who needed me more than these two little beings with their precious, upturned faces, their ready smiles and peels of gleeful hilarity. *Where else was it more important*

(or wonderful) to be than right here? It was almost blasphe-
mous to say things like this in the climate in which I raised
Marina, and Alex, where fierce independence and having everything you need inside of you were the ideas in vogue. But, for
me, it just wasn't true. Everything I needed simply wasn't inside of me. Outside of me, in the form of Brandt, Marina, and
Alex, were people so very important to my sense of well-being
and of leading a meaningful, purposeful life. People to matter
to. These little beings, with their ten fingers and ten toes, with
Brandt's and my DNA swirled around like a kaleidoscope inside of them; these were my kids, my heart, God in the form of
Marina, Alex, and Brandt. I didn't want to give up this moment
and now science is proving that I shouldn't. That the sweet attunement we shared, falling in and out of love and connection
a thousand times a day, the back and forth of our mutual dance
of mothering and childing all wove the neural threads that com-
posed the blueprint from which they would build throughout
life. All those moments counted. They were as important as
they felt.

This capacity to form caring, attuned, and loving bonds between parent and child is what forms an important part of the
template for later relationships. That is what children carry in
their own hearts long after the parent is gone. This experience
of loving and being loved impacts how they choose a mate
and parent their own children. It is the bond that creates a
safe space to learn and grow and risk and gives meaning to
words like *love, hurt, reconciliation,* and *connectedness.* That
makes discipline meaningful and tolerable; that inspires us to
be responsible, moral human beings.

And when we spend time with our children, we naturally help
them to be people we enjoy being around. Then they will eventually fall in line because they want to stay connected with us
and we with them. We will naturally make the myriad of little
adjustments that intimate relating requires. And if we truly feel
they light up the room, they will internalize this feeling and it,
too, will manifest in them over time. If they are important to

us, they will feel valuable and worthy and will naturally want to be the kind of people who bring something good to this world.

I have lived long enough to recognize that the hard work you put in when your children are young pays off for the rest of their lives and yours. Now's the time.

Over the years I have noticed that children who come from happy homes have a softness to their faces, a certain plasticity, or ability to flow with the subterranean rhythms of the moment, a readiness for what life might bring forth. As if, just beneath their skin, there vibrates a quiet self-confidence and a subtle joy, a willingness to meet and greet life on its own terms. When you see a child with a hard face, don't look to them, look further to see if the emptiness on their face reflects the emptiness that enfolds them when they walk through the door of their homes. They are wearing a mask to cover up their yearning for what's missing, that's all. Children who grow up in homes where there is genuine love and care wear that on their faces. And if there is spirituality, real spirituality, not the kind that is stuck in verbosity but the kind that expresses itself through meaningful and attuned action, then love and humor will likely follow naturally. Because in this home there is a reverence for life, a true and enduring embracing of the mystery.

Bibliography

Amen, Daniel G. *Change Your Brain, Change Your Life: The Breakthrough Program for Conquering Anxiety, Depression, Obsessiveness, Anger, and Impulsiveness*. New York: Times Books, 1998.

Axline, Virginia Mae. *Play Therapy*. New York: Ballantine Books, 1969.

Bard, Arthur S. and Mitchell G. Bard. *The Complete Idiot's Guide to Understanding the Brain*. Indianapolis: Alpha, 2002.

Blum, Deborah. *Love at Goon Park: Harry Harlow and the Science of Affection*. Cambridge, Mass.: Perseus, 2002.

Brazelton, T. Berry, and Bertrand G. Cramer. *The Earliest Relationship: Parents, Infants, and the Drama of Early Attachment*. Reading, Mass.: Addison-Wesley, 1990.

Corsini, Raymond J. *Encyclopedia of Psychology*. 2nd ed. New York: John Wiley & Sons, 1994.

Damasio, Antonio. *The Feeling of What Happens: Body and Emotion in the Making of Consciousness*. New York: Harcourt Brace, 1999.

Dayton, Tian. *The Living Stage: A Step-by-Step Guide to Psychodrama, Sociometry and Experiential Group Therapy*. Deerfield Beach, Fla.: Health Communications, 2005.

Dayton, Tian. *The Magic of Forgiveness: Emotional Freedom and Transformation at Midlife*. Deerfield Beach, Fla.: Health Communications, 2003.

Dossey, Larry. *Be Careful What You Pray For — What We Can Do About the Unintentional Effects of Our Thoughts, Prayers, and Wishes*. San Francisco: Harper San Francisco, 1997.

Dossey, Larry. *Healing Words: The Power of Prayer and the Practice of Medicine*. San Francisco: Harper San Francisco, 1993.

Elkind, David. *The Hurried Child: Growing Up Too Fast Too Soon*. 3rd ed. Cambridge, Mass.: Perseus, 2001.

Geary, David C. *Male, Female: The Evolution of Human Sex Differences*. Washington, D.C.: American Psychological Association, 1998.

Gellatly, Angus, and Oscar Zarate. *Mind and Brain for Beginners*. Cambridge: Icon, 1998.

Goldman, Robert M., with Ronald Klatz and Lisa Berger. *Brain Fitness: Anti-Aging Strategies for Achieving Super Mind Power*. New York: Doubleday, 1999.

Greenspan, Stanley I. *Building Healthy Minds: The Six Experiences That Create Intelligence and Emotional Growth in Babies and Young Children*. Cambridge, Mass.: Perseus Books, 1999.

Greenspan, Stanley I., and Nancy Thorndike Greenspan. *First Feelings: Milestones in the Emotional Development of Your Baby and Child.* New York: Viking, 1985.

Guindon, Mary H. "Feminist Therapy: What's It All About?" *Selfhelp Magazine* (2002). Online at *www.selfhelpmagazine.com/articles/women/femther.html*.

Gurwitch, Robin H., et al. "Reactions and Guidelines for Children Following Trauma/Disaster." Accessed online at *www.apa.org/practice/ptguidelines.html*.

Harlow, Harry F. "The Nature of Love." Address of the President at the sixty-sixth Annual Convention of the American Psychological Association, Washington, D.C., August 31, 1958. First published in *American Psychologist* 13, 573–685. Available online at *http://psychclassics.yorku.ca/Harlow/love.htm*.

Howard, Pierce J. *The Owner's Manual for the Brain: Everyday Applications from Mind-Brain Research.* Austin, Tex.: Bard Press, 2000.

Johnston, Victor S. *Why We Feel: The Science of Human Emotions.* New York: Perseus Books, 1999.

Kotulak, Ronald. *Inside the Brain: Revolutionary Discoveries of How the Mind Works.* Kansas City, Mo.: Andrews and McMeel, 1996.

LeDoux, Joseph. *The Emotional Brain: The Mysterious Underpinnings of Emotional Life.* New York: Simon & Schuster, 1996.

LeDoux, Joseph. *The Synaptic Self: How Our Brains Become Who We Are.* New York: Viking, 2002.

Levine, Peter A., with Ann Frederick. *Waking the Tiger: Healing Trauma: The Innate Capacity to Transform Overwhelming Experiences.* Berkeley, Calif.: North Atlantic Books, 1997.

Lewis, Thomas, Fari Amini, and Richard Lannon. *A General Theory of Love.* New York: Vintage Books, 2001.

Lyness, Karen S., and Michael K. Judiesch, "Are Female Managers Quitters? The Relationships of Gender, Promotions, and Family Leaves of Absence to Voluntary Turnover." *Journal of Applied Psychology* 86, no. 6 (December 2001): 1167–78? Also see online *www.apa.org/monitor/apr02/dispels.html*.

Montessori, Maria. *Dr. Montessori's Own Handbook.* Mineola, N.Y.: Dover Publications, 2005.

Montessori, Maria. *The Montessori Method.* Mineola, N.Y.: Dover Publications, 2002.

Montessori, Maria. *Spontaneous Activity in Education.* New York: Schocken Books, 1965.

Moreno, J. L. *Psychodrama.* Vol. 1. Beacon, N.Y.: Beacon House Press, 1946.

Northrup, Christiane. "The Mother of All Wake-Up Calls." *Today,* April 1, 2002.

Northrup, Christiane. *The Wisdom of Menopause: Creating Physical and Emotional Health and Healing during the Change.* New York: Bantam, 2001.

Ornish, Dean. *Love and Survival: The Scientific Basis for the Healing Power of Intimacy.* New York: HarperCollins, 1998.

Ornstein, Robert, and Charles Swencionis. *The Healing Brain: A Scientific Reader.* New York: Guilford Press, 1990.

Partenheimer, David. "Breast Cancer Patients Who Actively Express Their Emotions Do Better Emotionally and Physically, Says New Study." APA Press Release, October 22, 2000; *www.apa.org/releases/canceremotion.html.*

Peeke, Pamela. "What Menopause May Mean to You." *Today,* April 2, 2002.

Pennebaker, James W. *Opening Up: The Healing Power of Expressing Emotions.* New York: Guilford Press, 1997.

Pert, Candace B. *Molecules of Emotion: Why You Feel the Way You Feel.* New York: Simon & Schuster, 1999.

Piaget, Jean. *Intelligence and Affectivity: Their Relationship during Child Development.* Palo Alto, Calif.: Annual Reviews, 1981.

Rocha do Amaral, Júlio, and Jorge Martins de Oliveira. "Limbic System: The Center of Emotions." Online at *www.healing-arts.org/n-r-limbic.htm.*

Rosenthal, Norman E., *The Emotional Revolution: How the New Science of Feelings Can Transform Your Life.* New York: Citadel Press/Kensington Publishing, 2002.

Russell, Peter. *The Brain Book.* New York: Dutton, 1979.

Schore, Allan N. *Affect Regulation and the Origin of the Self: The Neurobiology of Emotional Development.* Hillsdale, N.J.: L. Erlbaum Associates, 1994.

Schore, Allan N. *Affect Regulation and the Repair of the Self.* Forthcoming from Guilford Press.

Smith, Deborah. "Major National Studies of Women's Health Are Providing New Insights." *Monitor on Psychology* 33, no. 5 (May 2002); *www.apa.org/monitor/may02/studies.html.*

Solms, Mark. "Towards an Anatomy of the Unconscious." *Journal of Clinical Psychoanalysis* 5 (1996): 331–67.

Stern, Daniel N. *The Interpersonal World of the Infant: A View from Psychoanalysis and Developmental Psychology.* New York: Basic Books, 1985.

Stern, Daniel N., and Nadia Bruschweiler-Stern, with Alison Freeland. *The Birth of a Mother: How the Motherhood Experience Changes You Forever.* New York: Basic Books, 1998.

Taylor, Shelley E., et al. "Biobehavioral Responses to Stress in Females: Tend-and-Befriend, Not Fight-or-Flight." *Psychological Review* 107, no. 3 (July 2000): 411–29.

Thagard, Paul, and Allison Barnes. "Emotional Decisions." *Proceedings of the Eighteenth Annual Conference of the Cognitive Science Society.* Hillsdale, N.J.: Erlbaum, 1996, 426–29.

Thoresen, Carl E. "Spirituality and Health: Is There a Relationship?" *Journal of Health Psychology* 4, no. 3 (1999): 291–300.

Tronick, Edward Z., et al. "Dyadically Expanded States of Consciousness and the Process of Therapeutic Change." *Infant Mental Health Journal* 19 (1998): 290–99.

Vaillant, George E. *Aging Well: Surprising Guideposts to a Happier Life from the Landmark Harvard Study of Adult Development.* Boston: Little, Brown, 2002.

Van der Kolk, Bessel A., ed. *Psychological Trauma.* Washington, D.C.: American Psychiatric Press, 1987.

Werner, Emmy E. "Children of the Garden Island." *Scientific American* 260 (1990): 106–11.

Wolin, Steven J., and Sybil Wolin. *The Resilient Self: How Survivors of Troubled Families Rise above Adversity.* New York: Villard Books, 1993.

Acknowledgments

This book was Senior Editor Roy M. Carlisle's idea. A nice idea, I thought. Full of a father's love for his own three daughters, a minister's love for his flock, and a book editor's knowledge of what is missing in the marketplace. When Roy asked me to write a book on how I taught my own kids emotional literacy using stories from their childhood, a book on conscious mothering, how could I say anything but yes? How could I miss the chance to write down all of the funny, heart-warming, and meaningful stories that made up our lives together? Add to that the opportunity to appraise new moms of the incredible research that is flooding the psychological scene not only on the critical importance of motherhood but also on just why and how our mothering shapes our children and yes, the answer is yes. So first I wish to thank my friend and generator of this book, Roy M. Carlisle. This was a lovely idea. I hope we do more.

Next I want to acknowledge my husband, Brandt, and our children, Marina and Alex Dayton. You have already met them thoroughly in the pages of this book. You know that they define the very shape and texture of my heart. I thank them for their generous permission in allowing me to write this book. Even though I am sure none of them loved the idea of having their personal moments written down in black and white, they were willing to allow me to go ahead and to trust that I would use at least some discretion in what I did and didn't say.

Next I want to acknowledge my own mother and father, Kosta and Elaine Barbatsis. I write this because it feels like my parents' names. Mom went on to marry Walt Walker, who for thirty years was a wonderful stepdad, and just before his death Dad married Alice, who was equally kind. But here I take literary license and list them side by side, as they are listed in my own DNA. These are the people who raised me, who loved me into being, laughed at my silly jokes, ooohed and ahhhed in a way that made me feel there was no one on earth quite like

160

me and cared for me until I could learn to care for myself. To them I owe so much, all that we owe to parents and that we repay only really by passing it forward. In addition to my mother, my father was very nourishing and attentive. So I wish the reader to understand that mothering can also come from a father and that to be mothered by a father is a deeply holding and very strengthening experience. My grandparents Chris and Anna Legeros were part of the pillars of our Greek church and the pillars of my life. Without them well — I cannot imagine a world without them, so crucial were they to my life, to my sense of who I was and am today. They were the very best and Grammie was the kind of grandmother who would bless and sustain any child's life. My aunts and uncles were, like good Greeks, very involved in my life and I can't picture growing up without them and their kids, namely my wonderful, zany, smart and much loved cousins. We are richly blessed. My in-laws and our children's grandparents Bruce and Ruth Dayton and Gwen and Lee MacPhail, who continued to raise me into adulthood and provide the love and structure that formed our children's inner beings, how can I thank you enough for all you have given all of us? And we have had the good fortune of filling out our worlds and our children's worlds with aunts, uncles, and cousins. We have been so lucky to have so many who are so very important to Marina and Alex and to us. My sisters, Kutzi and Eve, and my brother, Nick, and Brandt's sisters, Lucy and Anne, and his brother, Mark, and their children, Marina and Alex's wonderful cousins who they love so very much, have given them arms to grow up in, people who have a special interest in who they become and carry the memories of who they were from birth. Thank you for being here, for them and for us. You mean so much. And now for our friends. We have lived away from where we grew up and so have formed friendships with wonderful families with whom we raised our children. Our friends have come to be an extended family for us, and we love them dearly. We feel so lucky to have such good and close friends in both New York and Pawling. We thank you for being such beautiful, vibrant colors in the fabric of our lives. And last but never,

ever least are my mom friends. You know who you are. We have raised our children together, had a thousand and one conversations about each and every aspect of their lives, worn out countless pairs of tennis shoes walking through the park, drunk endless cups of tea solving the problems of their worlds, and held each other's hands as we walked gingerly through the mysterious journey of our children's hearts, minds, and lives, where angels fear to tread. Through motherhood.

You I thank in a very special way.

About the Author

Tian Dayton, PhD, TEP, holds a master's degree in educational psychology and a doctorate in clinical psychology, and she is a twice certified Montessori teacher for ages eighteen months to five years and ages five to twelve. Dr. Dayton is a fellow of the American Society of Psychodrama, Sociometry, and Group Psychotherapy (ASGPP), a board certified trainer of the method, winner of the society's scholar's award, and executive editor of the field's academic journal, and she sits on the professional standards committee. She is also the director of the New York Psychodrama Training Institute at Caron, New York. Tian spent eight years teaching psychodrama at New York University. Tian is a board member of the National Association for Children of Alcoholics. She has authored over fifteen books, including *Affirmations for Parents, Forgiving and Moving On, The Magic of Forgiveness, Journey through Womanhood, Heartwounds, Trauma and Addiction, The Quiet Voice of Soul, The Soul's Companion,* and others listed at the beginning of this book. Dr. Dayton has been a guest expert on NBC, CNN, and MSNBC, and has appeared with Montel, Rikki Lake, John Walsh, Geraldo, and on numerous radio programs.

Tian lives in Manhattan and Upstate New York with Brandt, her husband of thirty years, and near Marina, who lives in New Haven, Connecticut, and Alex, who lives in New York City.

For further information on Dr. Dayton's books, workshops, blog, and up-to-date research on psychological issues or to receive a free affirmation daily in your e-mail log on to *tiandayton.com.* or *drdayton.com.*

Log on to *modernmothering.com* for:

- FAQs on emotional literacy, emotional intelligence, and sound emotional development
- Further information on floor time
- Suggestions and guidelines on how to start your own mom support group

- Ideas on how to set up your child's room and how to create a kid-friendly world
- Kids' Corner: scrapbooking, cooking together, and creating a kid-friendly environment
- Moms' Corner: Tips for Mom, self-care, moms' journal
- Recent research on psychological issues
- Dr. Dayton's e-letter
- Your daily affirmation to get the day off to an inspired start

A Word from the Editor

I have waited many years for this to happen. This book, I mean, and working with Tian to publish one of her new books. Back in the 1990s I was introduced to Tian Dayton by a wonderful book editor who wanted me to help out with the editing of a new book by Tian. It was being produced by Dr. Dayton's longtime publisher, and again she was taking on a subject — the impact of unresolved trauma and grief on relationships — that was dear to my heart. It is an odd thing to have dear to one's heart I admit, but after years of publishing books in the area of recovery, trauma, and abuse at HarperSanFrancisco I was still convinced that these books were changing people's lives, and I wanted to be a part of it. My introduction to the owners of her company had led to this freelance opportunity, and when I found out that it would be one involving a new book from Tian titled *HeartWounds,* I jumped at the chance.

Why I jumped at the chance was an easy question to answer. First, Tian was a thoughtful and elegant writer. Second, she was working in the field in which I was doing another graduate degree, and it meant that I would have another aspect of my education greatly enhanced. Finally, everyone I knew who had met her raved about what a wonderful person she was. And that praise came from her company editor also, which meant a lot to me because editors who have done more than one book with an author usually know much more than anyone realizes about that author.

So I jumped in with both feet, and in her Acknowledgments for *HeartWounds,* Tian says, Roy "helped to yank, cajole, pull, and encourage this book out of me. . . . " But it was all so much fun that I looked forward to the day when I could work with Tian again as editor and publisher. We kept in touch over the years and dreamed about that opportunity.

In this instance the book was partly my idea, and I say partly because Tian is someone who has ideas for books floating through her brain like most of us have fantasies about chocolate or sex. So no doubt she was talking about a book on mothering in some form, and I said she ought to do that book, or some such kind of remark. So, of course, she did. When Tian does a book she just starts writing. And all kinds of "stuff" starts flowing out. It really is rather an amazing process to watch. She has done it so often now that she doesn't really worry about what will be in the book and what won't. She can just write, which she obviously enjoys immensely, and then revise and edit to the form desired. With this memoir about parenting and emotional literacy that form came in fits and starts because she had so much to say we could have filled many books. And the form gave us fits even right down to the wire before the book went to press. Again that is half the fun with Tian because she just doesn't give up until she has what she wants and what she thinks is right for a book.

This is a more personal book in some ways than her other books, although Tian always writes authentically out of her real-life knowledge and expertise. But in this instance she is including her whole family, so that really is more personal. She has obviously been a devoted and thoughtful mother, and it shows in the life and vitality within her family. I know I would have loved to have Tian for a mother even if she was always lost in thought about another book and obsessively pounding away at the keyboard. Actually I am impressed by how much she has done in her life even though she spent hour upon hour devoted to just teaching her children how to say what they feel and feel what they say. That is a phrase that should guide all of our lives. Especially as adults when the temptation is to neglect our feelings and the expression of them because we are all so busy. So to all the mothers who need another good reason to just "be" with your children, this book is a tribute to you and to what you do every day. We hope you continue to do this "work" even though you live in a culture where it is never valued as it should be. And all the children said, "Amen."

Roy M. Carlisle
Senior Editor

Of Related Interest

Dr. Keith W. Frome
WHAT NOT TO EXPECT
A Meditation on the Spirituality of Parenting

The multi-million-selling series What to Expect When You're Expecting tries to take the guesswork and fear out of being a parent by offering parents checklists, tips, and timelines for how to know what's coming next in a child's life.

Dr. Keith Frome admits that he and his wife love the What to Expect series. But as a professional educator, headmaster of a K-8 private school, and parent of two boys, he sees every day how children surprise us, frustrate us, and simply refuse to follow the checklist we prepared for them.

In *What Not to Expect,* Dr. Frome takes us through dozens of things families experience every day — winning and losing, eating, falling down, pooping — and shows how each of these catch us offguard. Part of being a parent is that we don't know what to expect. We need to embrace the disappointments and delightful surprises as the spiritual heart of parenthood.

Written as a complement to the Expecting series, *What Not to Expect* is thoughtful and humorous, drawing from Dr. Frome's Ivy League education and his vast knowledge of the world's spiritual and religious traditions.

0-8245-2282-6, $17.95, paperback

Of Related Interest

Margaret Smith
WHAT WAS I THINKING?
How Being a Standup
Did Nothing to Prepare Me
to Be a Single Mother

"Margaret Smith, blithely disregarding the conventional wisdom that female comics must labor within proscribed borders, has gone her own way." What the *New York Times* wrote about Smith's award-winning stand-up routine is also true of Smith's new book. In this hilarious romp, one of America's senior comedic writers describes what she thought it would be like — and what it was really like — to become a single mother!

0-8245-2285-0, $16.95, paperback

Please support your local bookstore,
or call 1-800-707-0670 for Customer Service.

For a free catalog, write us at

THE CROSSROAD PUBLISHING COMPANY
16 Penn Plaza – 481 Eighth Avenue, Suite 1550
New York, NY 10001

Visit our website at
www.cpcbooks.com
All prices subject to change.

crossroad